Marty Hogan, LC SW

PROFESSIONALS PRAISE
M. CATHERINE RAY'S **I'M HERE TO HELP**
FOR HOSPICE WORKERS

"Catherine Ray's book is a treasure! Finally, a book that clearly summarizes vitally important listening and communication skills, not just for hospice workers, but for everyone. The book's format is 'reader-friendly' and could be used in a variety of training settings, including health care institutions, religious communities and businesses."
— Edward Holland
Coordinator of Spiritual Care and Grief Support
Methodist Hospital Hospice, Minneapolis
President, 1993 and 1994, Minnesota Hospice Organization

"This is the *best* guide I have seen! We will give each new volunteer a copy at our next hospice training."
— Anne L. Walker, LBSW Executive Director
Hospice of Marshall County, Guntersville, Ala.

"This clear brief volume, rich in helpful material about self-awareness and family dynamics for hospice workers, supplies many useful examples of initiating and sustaining verbal and listening interactions. It also lists useful references and suggestions for finding and developing reading and related resources."
— Madalon O'Rawe Amenta
Editor, *The Hospice Journal*

ALSO BY M. CATHERINE RAY

I'm Here to Help:
A Guide for Caregivers,
Hospice Workers,
and Volunteers

I'm With You Now

A GUIDE THROUGH INCURABLE ILLNESS FOR PATIENTS, FAMILIES, AND FRIENDS

M. Catherine Ray

BANTAM BOOKS

New York   Toronto   London

Sydney   Auckland

I'M WITH YOU NOW
A Bantam Book/July 1997
All rights reserved.

Library of Congress Cataloging-in-Publication Data

Ray, M. Catherine.
I'm with you now: a guide through incurable illness
for patients, families, and friends/
M. Catherine Ray.
p.   cm.
Includes bibliographical references.
ISBN 0-553-37801-5
1. Incurable diseases.   2. Care of the sick.   3. Terminal care.
4. Caregivers.   I. Title.
RC48.R38   1997
362.1'75—dc20   96-41070   CIP

Published simultaneously in the United States and Canada

Bantam Books are published by Bantam Books, a division of
Bantam Doubleday Dell Publishing Group, Inc. Its trademark,
consisting of the words "Bantam Books" and the portrayal of a
rooster, is Registered in U.S. Patent and Trademark Office and in
other countries. Marca Registrada. Bantam Books, 1540
Broadway, New York, New York 10036.

*For those of us who travel the currents of incurable illness
and for the people who care about us—
may we strive for the bonus vistas,
savor our floats in the shade, feel more passion
than terror through the rapids,
and find reasons to celebrate
the voyage.*

CONTENTS

PREFACE

·

"When I imagined something like this happening," I told my sister, "I always thought it would be like an avalanche. The world would come crashing down around me, I'd feel smothered and overwhelmed." I was talking about my husband's recent diagnosis of incurable cancer.

"But it's not like that at all. . . . It's so much slower, like we're in the middle of a murky river. Our feet are stuck in the mud and the water is slowly rising. So slowly, it's nerve-racking. And we can't get out. I only wonder if someone will be able to pull us out before the water covers our heads."

Well, it's some time later, and we haven't drowned. And the river still carries us. We weren't permanently stuck in the mud, but my family, like thousands of others, continues to be swept downstream by the currents of incurable illness.

We found ourselves in some sort of boat, in the middle of this river. It isn't clear how we got here, or why, and none of us had this particular nautical experience. This craft didn't come with instructions; it has taken some time to grow comfortable at the helm.

Our friends and loved ones are on the riverbanks—they call out encouragement to us; they shout questions and instructions. "What's it like out there?" they want to know. "You should be moving over to the left," they scream. "We'll go call for help!" Voices over water . . . sometimes so clear you can hear a whisper, sometimes muted and muffled. It's hard to talk, hard to hear. We float nearer, then farther away.

There are maddening times when our boat gets stuck in an eddy, spinning and stagnant, week after week as they nail down a diagnosis or deliberate over treatment. There are reflective times of watching the clouds while we gently float, times of calming conversations about our dreams and plans and deferments.

As time goes by, we grow more confident. We learn to move in sync as we navigate the currents. We feel strong and capable, alert and appreciative of this world and its beauties. As we take in the scenery, there are days when we feel positively joyous, even grateful for the gifts of this voyage.

Then come those places where the river grows intense. . . . It spills us over the rocks and rapids of relapse and complications. . . . Some of us keep our eyes wide open, others cower and bury our faces. All we can do is hang on to each other, terrified, and pray.

And always—even during the gentler times—we remain acutely aware we could capsize.

This is no earthshaking avalanche, over in fifteen seconds. It is a long, slow river journey—sometimes frustrating, sometimes frightening, sometimes even exhilarating.

ABOUT THIS BOOK

·

I'm With You Now is about the communication that occurs during a very special voyage—the journey through incurable illness. It is written for patients and their loved ones; it is also written for the doctors, nurses, school systems, co-workers, poker pals, and countless caring others who watch from the riverbanks.

When a family is swept up in the currents of incurable illness, we often struggle over what to say and how to say it. Social awkwardness can sabotage us. We scare ourselves into pulling away and remaining silent, shortchanging everyone of the chance to share this voyage. After all, this isn't a trip taken by just anybody; in fact, it's an experience of great magnitude. If we are involved with such a profound voyage, even indirectly, there is so much to learn by it—but only when we notice the scenery, dare to talk about it, and provide assistance when we're able.

I'm With You Now is offered as guidance. It highlights specific communication skills that enable us to take better control of the helm during this journey. Stories from other voyagers are sprinkled throughout, since it is instructive to hear from those who have already traveled downstream. These vignettes are stories I have been told and tales from my own experience. Details are altered and sources remain unidentified, not to "protect the innocent" but to acknowledge that such experiences are universal.

I began this book to help people "out there" with this experience. Halfway through its writing, my family suddenly found itself on a similar journey. It has since become even more vital to me that *all* parties make the most of this voyage, from the patients and loved ones careening through the currents, to the co-workers and casual acquaintances observing from shore.

I hope *I'm With You Now* helps travelers talk more and share their profound reactions and insights. Hopefully, it will urge onlookers to pay closer attention and offer more tangible support—perhaps even wade into the river themselves occasionally, providing caregiving respite the family may so desperately need. In short, I hope this book becomes a valuable map for a voyage that can often be treacherous—and also extraordinary.

· 1 ·
FINDING OURSELVES
IN THE RIVER

- **You or someone you care about has been diagnosed with an incurable illness.** It's as if you found yourself suddenly adrift, caught up by some current you can't control. And you wonder, how did *this* happen? Who picked me to go on this voyage? And why? And what if I can't disembark before crashing over the falls?

- **This excursion includes more than one passenger.** The boat carries the patient, but also a close circle of loved ones. On the banks, others are watching. The boat gets reeled in by the medical team; they try to supply provisions, but sometimes the storehouses are empty. Many different people are affected by this journey. Each has a different perspective about it.

- For anyone involved in this situation, it is important to remember one thing: *incurable* does not mean lethal. *Incurable* **does not mean terminal.**

- *Incurable* only means that once a disease has progressed to a certain point, it can't be stopped because it does not respond to the available treatments we have . . . today. **Remember, most diseases were once considered incurable**.

- **Research is occurring even as I write this, at hospitals and clinics and universities all over the world. Even more knowledge will be available by the time you read this.** Perhaps you know someone who had polio. Rheumatic fever. Tuberculosis. Less than a decade ago, Hodgkin's disease was considered terminal; today some cases are considered curable.

- **The progress of a disease is perhaps more important than its immediate curability.** Many incurable diseases develop slowly, so that lifestyle changes are gradual. And a slow progression increases the chance that an effective treatment will be uncovered, and perhaps even *cure* someone who was called terminal at the time of initial diagnosis.

- **A factor in illness is its visibility.** For example, some cancers occur at skin level—they are hard to ignore. Others do more internal damage—it is easier for patients to deny the illness, and onlookers may not be as sensitive because they can't see it.

The strangest thing is that, for the most part, I look fine. Healthy. Just the same as ever. This little tumor, it's only the size of a quarter, and it's way deep inside. Sometimes even I can't believe I'm walking around with something that might kill me in a few years.

Now, when I watch the guy behind the counter at the grocery store or the ticket taker at the movies, I think about all the people they talk to in a month, and how many of those people are dying, too. Probably hundreds. If we realized, we'd all feel uncomfortable. But I guess death is sometimes invisible, at least in the beginning. It doesn't always show up on the outside. It's almost like it waits awhile, giving me a chance to get used to the idea, before the rest of the world has to look at me and be forced to face it, too.

- **The journey through incurable illness is intense.** We're in a place few of our fellow human beings truly see, even when the disease is visible to the eye. This ride can be lonely and hard, sometimes even terrifying. Not everyone survives. But the scenery is phenomenal, almost surrealistic. We are carried toward new perspectives and insights, some so profound we can scarcely describe them.

- **True, no one asks for this excursion. But once we're here, we have a choice.** We can cower in the bottom of the boat with our eyes closed, praying that someone else handles the helm. Or we can sit up straight, grab an oar, and open our eyes to the incredible vistas around us.

- **Never forget, incurability isn't necessarily fatal.** And regardless the ultimate destination of this journey, there's something to be said for keeping our eyes open during the ride.

NOTES

NAVIGATING THE
CHANGING CURRENTS

- **The experience of illness brings a simple piece of wis-dom—everything changes. Nothing stays the same.** People who live with incurable illness know about change at a profound level. They live it, they breathe it, and believe it or not, there even comes a day when they can actually appreciate it.

- **For one thing, this awareness of change helps us celebrate our lives on a moment-by-moment basis.** We no longer take the world for granted. And we will forever find more beauty and depth and meaning in this world than most. This is our merit badge.

- **Earning this merit badge requires us to cope with changes others can only imagine**—an altered financial picture, a hospital bed where the dining room table used to be, loss of hair, a friend who no longer acts like one, becoming housebound. We will find, in addition, that enumerating these changes is comforting.

- **Some changes are permanent, others are recurring. A perma-nent change transforms things irreversibly.** An earthquake is one example; terrain heaves, never to return to its original geologi-cal layering. Losing a parent is another example; the family will never be quite like it was before.

- **A recurring change is really temporary,** a movement from one state to another, but things will eventually return to their original state. The circle of seasons is one example. Or, chemotherapy may cause hair loss, but eventually the hair will restore itself.

- **Incurable illness incorporates both types of change. Perma-nent:** perhaps the patient can no longer drive or walk without as-sistance, altering the very structure of our daily lives. **Recurring:**

a caregiver has bad days followed by good days. Or, radiation causes patient fatigue, but eventually the energy level returns to its previous state.

- **Both types of change require different methods of coping. Permanent change can require drastic adjustment. But once the changes and resulting adjustments are accomplished, the transition is complete.** For example, if a patient's leg must be amputated during treatment, changes in lifestyle and mobility will also occur. But once the patient becomes accustomed to wheelchair and prosthesis, she's progressed far beyond the original shock of this change and the tremendous efforts she's made to adjust to it. And she never again has to return to those earlier, painful stages.

- **Recurring change can require extra patience and endurance. It happens time after time, usually in patterns of predictable duration. It may not be as radical or life-altering as permanent change, but it *never goes away*.** For instance, your sister is always nauseous for three full days after treatment, then she's better. Or perhaps your mother was first diagnosed on Valentine's Day, and every year when that holiday arrives you can't help but think about this and be saddened.

- **Permanent change requires *flexibility*. Recurring change requires *stamina*.** Once we can name the type of change we are experiencing, we can adjust our energies and responses accordingly.

- **Different people in your circle will have a variety of responses to any particular change.** For example, now that your mother is incurably ill, your sister grows morose every holiday season; yet you feel relatively unaffected by these cycles. Or perhaps your niece views a nursing home as the next logical step for her father, while you feel this permanent change would be unnecessary.

- **Perceptions about the source of illness are another important factor because we often equate *source* with *responsibil-***

ity. We want to know, what was it that caused this illness to wreak havoc with our family? Where did this disease come from, and who can we hold accountable? **When a disease is perceived as preventable through changed behavior, anger and resentment are likely.** For instance, we can be harshly judgmental when a parent knowingly risks passing on a hereditary illness—"Why didn't they adopt, instead?!" Or, if a loved one smoked three packs a day for thirty years and now she's dying of lung cancer, it is nearly impossible not to blame her for her illness, subtly or otherwise. And we are all aware of people who believe that patients with AIDS somehow deserve the disease.

I was helping a family from my church—the father had lung cancer. But he would never admit it. He wasn't comfortable talking about his illness at all—he seemed more afraid than many people I've volunteered with. One day his wife told me privately that he'd promised to quit smoking his whole life but he'd never been able to do it. "He supposedly quit about three years ago, but he still sneaks them in the garage. I don't know why he thinks I can't tell, but I've never said anything. So that's why he won't ever talk about it. He feels guilty. And dammit, he should feel guilty."

- **Some families are ambushed by a serious illness—it storms on them with no rational cause, correlation, or warning—the family just becomes a one-in-a-million statistic.** Members of this family might question their faith and struggle to make sense of their world. They may feel especially resistant to the lifestyle changes they must now make.

- **Once the family recognizes their individual perceptions about the source of this illness and its changes, they need to look carefully, talk about it, and then let it go.** We must avoid entangling our circle of loved ones in blame and guilt. We mustn't spend any more time than necessary angry at each other or at the world and its randomness. Our energies are far too valuable to be wasted in this way.

- **One of the biggest demands of this journey is the family's ability to deal with major changes that are simultaneously permanent and recurring—the changes of remission, relapse, remission, relapse, remission.** The disease is treated, it gets under control. The disease returns, sometimes with new presentations and life-altering consequences. Symptoms are treated and once again controlled. Illness returns again. And so on.

- **People experiencing incurable illness know precisely what the words *remission* and *relapse* mean.** They are acutely aware their disease cannot be eliminated from their body; in short, they can't be cured, at least not today. But with treatment, often they can live symptom-free, for years and years. For incurably ill people and their loved ones, there is no longer an all-out attempt to "beat this disease." Rather, the goal becomes symptom-free survival.

- **When incurable patients have successfully completed treatment—and happily gone into remission—many of their friends and family members talk to them as if a purely permanent change has occurred, as if they have been cured.** These friends and family say things like, "We're so glad you beat that thing!" or "Sure is nice to be over with all that." The patient or loved one might nod and smile, and for the most part he lets these remarks slide, but he thinks to himself, "You haven't got a clue what this is like for us. We're still in the middle of all this and we're petrified."

- **We help our incurable friends and loved ones when we remember there's a huge difference between remission and cure.** Not that we ought to dwell on this subject, or even bring it up directly, but at least we can be sensitive to the fact that our loved one's struggles with this illness are not necessarily over.

- **Relapses can be terrifying.** The boat suddenly plummets over the falls. It's a wild ride and we hang on for dear life, uncertain we'll land right side up. When we make it through these episodes without capsizing we're immensely grateful—but in regaining our bearings we sometimes find we've lost something, too, as if a precious piece of cargo was tossed overboard during the rapids. For example, the patient didn't drown, and we're thankful. But we're saddened because she now requires a wheelchair.

- **Even if relapse never happens—and it won't for many of us—anyone experiencing incurable illness *fears* the symptoms returning. This fear never completely subsides.** For most families, two main effects are in place, sometimes for decades; these effects occur in loved ones, as well as patients:

  - **Heightened Body Awareness**—preoccupation with the illness, searching the body for evidence of the illness (sometimes obsessively), concerns about sexuality and fertility, scary episodes in which relapse symptoms turn out to be common infections or viruses

---

I think one of the hardest things for me is that I now worry about every little thing that happens to my husband's body. He gets these strange infections because the treatment was so hard on him—but then again, his particular disease is a little like AIDS in that it affects his immune system. So whenever anything happens to him, even a little bump or scratch, I immediately think, "Oh, my God, it's back." People probably think we should be calmer about his situation now, because he's been in remission a long time. But I don't think I've felt relaxed about his health for over eight years now. I could drive the whole family crazy if I'm not careful.

  - **Fear and Uncertainty about the Future**—concerns about leaving our family vulnerable, personal questions about the legacies we've left (see Signatures, p. 177), the possibility of facing death with all its mysteries, etc.

I'm actually not so afraid of the dying part, or what happens after. But deep down inside I always thought I'd be famous. And I'm not. Maybe that sounds conceited or cocky, but I honestly thought I'd have the chance to make my mark on the world.

So now, I don't really care to go to Europe. I don't want to learn how to drive race cars, or any of the other things I used to dream about. Instead, I just want to work as long and hard and well as I possibly can. And it isn't just because of the money or worrying about leaving things to my wife and kids. It's more because I'm really good at my job. I'm in my prime. And if I have a chance to be famous at all, it will probably be in my industry. I want them to remember me.

- **If a relapse has recently happened to the patient in your circle of loved ones, please remember—relapses are recurring changes, not necessarily permanent ones. The relapse often goes into remission,** too, just as the initial illness did. I know someone who has had eleven official relapses and remissions. It's been twenty-seven years since her initial diagnosis, and she's still counting. In those twenty-seven years, she's written two books, had six grandchildren, and her life experiences have brought incomparable insight to those she continues to touch. It hasn't been easy, but she's supremely happy and loves her life.

- **A relapse can bring on a very powerful emotional response, just as the initial diagnosis did.** For many patients, a relapse brings about acute feelings of failure. It's as if they feel personally responsible. They may experience feelings of guilt for "letting down their families." Helpful friends and medical professionals are careful to avoid saying things like, "She *failed* chemotherapy."

- **Many of the same feelings and fears experienced the first time will appear**—the numbness, the anger, the dread over the thought of new treatments, fears that treatments won't work, having to tell family and friends all over again.

I had worked in hospice for fifteen years when I was diagnosed with cancer myself. I thought I knew it all at first, and hospice philosophy has always taught me to be completely open and honest. I swore if this ever happened to me I'd tell people, I'd seek out support from others. And I did do that, in the beginning.

But when I relapsed, something changed—I didn't need to tell people. Oh, I told a few close friends and one sister, but the others I've chosen to leave in the dark. Their reactions were so huge and complicated the first time around. . . . I've already spent enough energy calming their fears. I just didn't feel like going through everyone else's turmoil. Maybe it sounds selfish, but I haven't told them because I don't need their support anymore. It really doesn't matter to me if they have up-to-the-minute details.

I don't feel dishonest, because everyone I care about has known I was incurable from the start. And if I don't have as much time left, I don't want every conversation I have to start with the question, "So, Mary, how are you doing?"

- **Yet, it's different this time, too.** The waiting for results may not seem quite so excruciating. The family doesn't feel obliged to tell everybody—or they'll relay the information differently, based on how their network reacted the first time. **In short, the family now has experience with this illness.** They have already proved they can live with crisis and make tough decisions.

- **A major change occurs for some families who choose hospice care.** This can be a very difficult family decision. Hospice is a philosophy, not a particular place. It values the circle of life and views dying as a natural, normal part of human existence. Its focus is on the family, not just the patient. Hospice support is available—even free—to patients with a shortened prognosis (generally six months or less). Care frequently takes place in the patient's home, or sometimes in a special wing of a hospital, or perhaps in a stand-alone facility.

- **Hospice focuses on healing care—not cure.** The typical patient no longer receives disease-combating treatments. Instead, medical science is used for keeping the patient comfortable and alert, and able to enjoy a meaningful quality of life during these final months. (*An important point:* hospice nurses and physicians probably have more knowledge about pain relief than any other medical professional, including anesthesiologists. It could help to remember this later, even if your loved one never needs actual hospice care; you might want to contact a hospice for pain management information and referrals.)

- **Hospice care is more than medical care. The family is served by a team of professionals,** from nurses and home health aides to clergy and social workers, all bolstered by a committed corps of volunteers. The patient's family receives medical care and equipment (including free prescriptions), education and assistance with home care, twenty-four-hour access to practical/emotional/spiritual support, volunteers who provide respite, and more.

- **Unfortunately, the very word *hospice* carries some scary stigmas and implications.** Patients commonly say, "I know I'm eligible for hospice, my doctor even suggested it, but it seems like giving up. I'm not ready to call myself a hospice patient, yet." **This is a major frustration for hospice workers—and ultimately their patients—because they know from experience how much easier this journey can be if they are allowed to assist.** But often hospice is contacted only in the final weeks of illness, and there goes five months of patient care and family support, right down the drain.

I talked to a good friend just a few days before she died. She told me, "I know you kept telling me to find a hospice, and you know I kept putting you off. Well, I finally did it. And I have a wonderful hospice nurse named Wendy. I've known her less than two weeks and already she's helped me more than all my other doctors and nurses combined. You were right—I should have done this before. But at least I did it, I'm grateful for that."

- **Living with a limited prognosis is not easy—not physically, emotionally, or spiritually. If a family you care about travels these treacherous waters, gently encourage them to seek hospice help.** A hospice team eases the journey toward death without hastening it. Indeed, hospice helps the family celebrate life. Ask those who have experienced hospice in their own families; the majority say things like, "It wasn't an easy time, but somehow hospice made it *good*. We couldn't have done this without them." **Help patients and their loved ones change their predispositions toward the word *hospice*.**

- **Serious illness brings change in so many ways. Just as a patient can change physically—and sometimes drastically—week to week, she also changes spiritually and philosophically.** We do not see the "same" person today that we saw even four days ago. These philosophical and spiritual changes occur in loved ones, too.

- **Each friend and family member has a unique connection, each carries a unique perspective** regarding the incurable loved one. The private interpretations of this experience are as numerous as the people who are touched by it. And so are their changes and shifting priorities.

- **Travelers may discover that they prefer radically different courses.** For instance, a young man with an incurable illness might wish to work as hard and long as possible to provide for his family, while his wife prefers for him to cut back, get rest, and spend as much time together as possible.

- **The voyage might not feel as steady during those times when passengers are leaning in different directions.** But we can do a lot of rocking and meandering without making the boat capsize. **We can also change direction**—about treatment decisions, or living arrangements, or anything, even the medical team. Sure, we might have to paddle upstream for a while, but it's good to remember we can change our minds.

- **It is also essential to remind ourselves, "we are *more* than this illness."** It does permeate our family on an everyday basis, but we need to take care that it doesn't smother everything else we have together.

A new friend met my husband for the first time and they were immediately kindred spirits. She said later that it was so great to talk with him about music and art and politics; her exact words were "He's much more than his illness." And I thought to myself how hard it is for me to see beyond it—or maybe what I see is my fears about a future without him. But I look at him and my head screams "Cancer!" all the time. I told my friend that I now find myself thinking about her comment at least three times a day. I'll look at him and begin to think about what could happen, then I force myself to refocus—he's so much more than this illness.

- **People on this voyage are often surprised by their loved ones' changes, and especially by their out-of-character reactions.** For instance, a man who has been traditionally reserved about his fears and vulnerabilities suddenly starts sharing them openly. Or a person who has been fairly forthcoming suddenly becomes more guarded in her communication.

- **This is a powerful passage. It would *have* to change people.** And it is a big mistake to try to predict our reactions to the voyage. We have to be in the river before we know how the current affects us. We have to arrive at a particular tributary before we are able to choose it.

- **We may sometimes be overwhelmed** by the changing currents of this unplanned journey. At other times, we realize these changes have carried us toward priceless opportunities.

After my father was diagnosed, he became a completely different person. The change was incredible. No one could believe it. You know, he had always been a real corporate type, extremely successful, a real workaholic—no fluff about him, and not much time for anybody. But after he found out he was ill, he started making all kinds of new friends. He'd take people to their support group meetings, he'd drive them to their appointments. He was funny, and warm, and he had a love of life I'd never seen before. He said to me, "Katie, I can't even say I'm completely sorry this happened to me. . . . In so many ways, I feel better and more alive than I ever have. I'm only mad at myself for wasting so much time before now."

NOTES

3

BOUNDARIES

- **The wisest people recognize their boundaries on this journey. The ill person needs to be vocal about setting limits.** For example, it is not necessary for us to sit up and chat with an acquaintance if we'd rather rest alone. **For those of us who are close loved ones**—perhaps a spouse or child—we need to recognize that we are deeply involved in this disease. But we don't have the disease ourselves. **If we are a friend or acquaintance,** we can observe the suffering in our loved one's family and remain compassionate, without immersing ourselves. Avoid making this a vicarious experience.

- **It helps to be wary of people who exhibit unhealthy dependencies;** they are prime candidates for boundaries problems—which won't be very helpful to the family.

- **Boundaries (and exceeding them) appear in different ways:**
  - **Time:** when an overly demanding patient asks us to do just one more thing
  - **Belongings:** when a home-care aide uses something of ours without asking; when a relative rearranges our kitchen to "make things easier to reach" without first asking permission
  - **Privacy:** when a friend interrupts the patient in the bath or bedroom without knocking; when a caregiver eavesdrops on a telephone conversation
  - **Feelings:** when a family member walks in on someone else's argument, immediately takes sides, and becomes vocal; when a friend tells us how we "should" be feeling

- **Space:** when a loved one tells you they feel uncomfortable unless you are always close by; when a home-care aide stands much closer to you than you'd like

- **Intimacy:** when a friend asks a patient highly personal questions; when an acquaintance or volunteer tells a caretaker more about himself than the caretaker wants to hear

- **Learn to say no.** When we are protecting our boundaries, we aren't even obligated to give a reason. Merely say:

  "I have to do some other things tomorrow; I won't have time."

  "My drawers are private—please ask if you need something."

  "I prefer the kitchen arranged the way it was before, please."

  "Please knock before coming into my bedroom."

  "This discussion involves only us, not you."

  "I prefer my own chair over here, thanks."

  "I don't care to talk about that part of my life."

- **Or, when someone probes or pushes past the point of comfort, just change the subject.**

- **Helpful friends remember that families establish appropriate boundaries differently.** In some families, the entire family walks around nude; in others, even married spouses don't look directly at each other's bodies. Some families lock doors; others don't. Some families discuss highly intimate subjects with each other; others don't. **Be prepared to interact with a family you care about on *their* terms,** though this might feel uncomfortable for us sometimes because the boundaries in our families are different.

- **It helps when we are aware of our own "unfinished business": the things we privately think and feel about illness, life and death, and why we think them.** Our own experience could negatively affect our relationship with the family if we aren't careful. For example, if we are secretly troubled by an important relationship that was never reconciled, we might inadvertently push an ill friend to reconcile with someone in *her* life—even though she really doesn't care to. **Unfinished business goes beyond one's perspective on illness.** For example, imagine that the patient's husband is alcoholic and we grew up in an alcoholic family. We need to take care that our own experience with chemical dependency doesn't negatively affect our interactions as we support this family.

• **Avoid becoming the family's therapist.** Are we being pulled in, such that we feel uncomfortable? Are we asked to referee disputes, for example? We need to tell them so tactfully. "You know, I think I'm in over my head here. Let's talk to some other people about this, too."

• **Just as important, we must avoid turning our own family and friends into *our* therapists.** When we live through the stresses of watching someone we care about grow progressively ill, we can quickly become obsessive with our other loved ones and overly demanding on our support system at home. Talk to others about these profound experiences, not just your spouse and best friends. Engage in other forms of self-care and stress release (see Therapies for Stress and Burnout, p. 139).

• **Good friends know they are exceeding their boundaries when**

  • they lose objectivity—for instance, becoming resentful rather than merely irritated toward a cranky patient or a particular fussy family member (even if they don't openly express it)

  • their stress increases—they feel emotionally on edge with their other family and friends

  • they find themselves thinking about the patient and the patient's loved ones too frequently

  • they feel like they want to take over

  • they feel like the patient/family welfare is *their* responsibility

- they feel confused about whose feelings are whose, such as a best friend becoming openly antagonistic toward the patient's grown daughter because "she isn't doing enough to support *us* in this difficult situation"

- **Without boundaries, we'll either drown each other or fail to connect entirely.**

NOTES

4

SHARING THE STORY,
FINDING SUPPORT

- **When news of our situation gets out, we suddenly find that hundreds of people around us are meandering through life with incurable illnesses.** Fellow travelers on this voyage frequently approach a patient and loved ones during the illness. Acquaintances step forward, even strangers. All come forth to share their common bond. "When I heard about your sister's illness, I just had to say something. I was treated for breast cancer myself, five years ago." Or, "I heard about your husband. When I was thirty-four, I was diagnosed with lupus." **Support certainly comes from those we know and love. It also comes from complete strangers.** •

Something that really shocked me was how many people are walking around with very serious sicknesses. I never realized this until I got sick myself, then all of a sudden people I barely knew and sometimes even total strangers started opening up to me. It was like I was magnetized. I'm not sure how it happens, but you just find yourself talking about it with complete strangers who "have been there." This one survived testicular cancer, that one has lymphoma, another has colitis. Even the guy who sold me my computer—only twenty-five years old and already a three-year cancer survivor. On the one hand, I sometimes feel like I can't get away from this. On the other, I'm really comforted to know I'm not alone. Lots of people are going through what I am. I just never knew it before.

- **Even people *without* experience may come forward—perhaps total strangers.** Some of these conversations are helpful and reassuring. Others might make us angry or hurt our feelings. Their questions may seem bold; their comments may feel invasive. **And sometimes, specific people we wish would come forward won't.** Maybe they can't. Maybe they don't know what to say or do.

- **Our friends stay away and can't offer us support for many reasons.** Sometimes they are afraid of breaking down themselves. Sometimes their own lives are so complicated or difficult, they have no energy to help us with ours.

- **And sometimes—we need to admit this—we wear them out.** Face it, families living with incurable illness need to tell their stories . . . again, and again, and again. It is extremely tiring for our mothers and cousins and best friends to listen, again and again, especially as they are trying to cope with their own lives and losses.

I want to share my symptoms with my family. I want to tell them what this disease feels like, in and on my body. And it isn't always because it hurts. Sometimes I want to talk about it because it fascinates me, all these changes. But I don't always mention things. I'm never sure if they think I'm being informative or if they think I'm just complaining.

- Especially in the early stages, we need to avoid concerning ourselves about other people's reactions (or lack of reactions). **Try to take good from the support you have, and let the hurtful things wash away.**

- **When serious illness strikes, a surprising new role crops up for the patient and family—that of educator.** Family members become informed about their particular illness through experience and research, and they spend lots of time educating their less-involved loved ones.

- **Another major responsibility is shouldered by the patient and family: They spend tremendous energy calming fears and**

making others feel comfortable with the situation. This can be gratifying, but also frustrating and exhausting for the family.

My kids and I laugh about people with "puppy dog faces"—it's that look some people get when they ask how we are. We hate it, but we're learning to laugh at it. It's a mournful, pitiful look, and it frustrates me, because I can never tell these "puppy dog" people how we really are—I'm too busy trying to calm them down, so they'll wipe that horrid expression off their faces. If only people would ask about us without looking all "puppy dog" about it, maybe I could really tell them.

• **We need to share our story with others in order to gain their support. But the family quickly learns: Talking with some people can be helpful and comforting; talking to particular others only depletes their energies.** When the others we tell over-react, when they offer unsolicited advice, when they pity us, when they need us to provide reassurances we don't have, we soon find ourselves wishing we hadn't opened up to them at all.

• **What are the characteristics of a good support person?** If we asked patients and their loved ones this question, their list might look like this:

  • A supportive person listens, nurtures, and doesn't change the subject.

  • This person is flexible and patient.

  • It's a person who *offers* rather than waiting to be asked.

  • A supportive person is truthful, whose statements are tempered with tact and an excellent sense of timing.

  • You feel accepted by a supportive person, even with your flaws.

  • A supportive person encourages us to be our best and happiest, and provides the positive, gentle push we need to do this.

- It's a person who helps you clarify your problems, but talks about other things, too; a person who sees the whole you.

- A supportive person is available in all types of weather. They show up right when you need them to say "What can I do?" And when you tell them, they *do* it, even when you say, "Go away for a while. I can't talk about this now."

- A supportive person provides reassurance rather than asking for it.

- You feel their touch even when they are not present.

- **It's a heady list of requirements.** Most people have few loved ones or friends—if any—who could meet all these criteria. But if every friend could commit to doing even half of this list, the family's voyage would be so much easier.

- **Even for people who have a large network of personal support, there comes a time when it is *imperative* to step outside the immediate circle of family and friends to seek support elsewhere.** This is especially true if we are feeling more and more isolated, or if we seem stuck in some part of this process. If friends begin to change the subject, if they say "I've heard this before," if they begin to avoid us, it is essential to find others to whom we can tell our stories.

- **Support groups can offer tremendous help in providing an outlet.** It feels liberating to find a safe place where we can truthfully talk about our situation with others who have similar experiences. It normalizes the sometimes surreal world of incurable illness.

- **Support can be found in lots of formats.**
  1. Individual sessions with a therapist, counselor, minister, or others (especially helpful for someone who is stuck in some part of the process)
  2. Couples counseling (especially good for people with an ill child)

3. Family counseling (useful in sibling or parent illness)
4. Condition-specific organizations (for AIDS, lupus, cancer, etc.)
5. Situation-specific organizations (MADD, suicide, murder, etc.)
6. Bereavement groups (general or condition/situation-specific)
7. Any combination of the above formats

- Find help through your **hospital, hospice, church or temple,** or other organizations. Contact your **local, city, county, and state government** office for any information about support that is available (even free) through various public agencies. Look in the **Yellow Pages under Social Services.** The **library** has reference books that list every national self-help organization, often with toll-free 800 numbers. Check out reputable **self-help clearinghouses** that maintain extensive lists of the nation's self-help programs and resources. Use the **Internet** to communicate with people all over the world who share your experience.

- **Families struggling to achieve spiritual calm could use a little outside help, but we build barriers toward seeking it.** We tell ourselves we are too busy, we fear the risks, we worry about confidentiality and the *shoulds* of our professional life, we fear we will fall apart during the sessions, we prefer to cope by denying the problem, the idea of needing a support group makes us feel inadequate or like we are failures, we fear giving up control.

- **And finding the right group or counselor isn't easy because it frequently takes more than one try to find the proper "fit."** Personalities need to mesh, and it is completely normal to feel uncomfortable in a new support setting at first. It takes time to build trust and find our niche, and it might be several sessions before we feel even remotely ready to open ourselves up to others. That's why it is a good idea to **reserve judgment for three full meetings.** If the group or counselor isn't meeting our needs by this time, we need to look for another, and we should expect to have to shop around for a while.

- **Looking for the right support group can be time-consuming and even scary, and sometimes we allow those feelings to stop us before we even begin.** *Don't give up.* The effort is worth it, and the benefits are many:

    - *Great comfort is gained when we share our stories with other people who are in a situation similar to ours.* It feels good to talk to another wife about having an ill husband; it feels good to talk to another kid about having a sick mom or dad. Talking with other patients and their families validates our experience, makes it real, and shows us we aren't crazy.

    - *Support group members learn new coping mechanisms from each other:* how one adjusts to a prosthesis, for instance, or recipes that calm the nausea of chemotherapy, or book recommendations, or perhaps agencies that offer financial or medical assistance.

    - *Exploring and clarifying ideas with others who share your role helps you better express yourself when you talk to your own family members.* For instance, first you work out your anger and anxieties about financial concerns with other spouses in your support group—then you figure out how to express these issues to your spouse (the patient).

    - *The family's network of support is greatly increased.*

    - *We learn we are not alone.*

- **And perhaps the biggest benefit is that "formal" support frees you to be a friend to the *others* you love.** Those friends care. They love the family and want to help. But truly, they can't possibly understand the intricacies of the family's experience—at least not the same way someone else does who more closely shares it.

- **Friends are generally grateful to a patient or loved one who takes the initiative to bring up the topic of the illness.** "Oh, I'm so glad you mentioned it," they say. "Of course I *wanted* to know how things are but I didn't feel I should ask." Or, "I've wanted to bring it up but I didn't know how." Patients and their close loved ones can help others over this awkwardness by offering information, when it seems appropriate.

• **As for the friends' role in lending support, one rule of thumb is that they *ask* for information rather than *provide* it.** For example, "I've heard about lung cancer but there are lots of different kinds, aren't there? What is it like for *YOU*?" is much more effective than "My aunt had lung cancer; they gave *her* radiation."

• **When friends decide to approach a patient or loved one about the family's situation, they need to consider the surroundings.** Is it a domain where the family might prefer to de-emphasize the illness (such as a child's school or the workplace)? Are other people within earshot? If so, perhaps a different time would be better.

I remember being approached in the lobby of my daughter's school, by a very warm and well-meaning woman. The problem was, there were about twenty other parents within earshot, too! We hadn't told my daughter's teachers yet. . . . We were still grappling with the news ourselves. Even though I eventually appreciated her gesture, at the time she made it I felt really awful—invaded and exposed.

• **The earliest stages of incurable illness are often hardest emotionally; the shock is so raw and the future seems so uncertain.** The waiting for test results and treatment recommendations can seem interminable. The agony is compounded because friends and acquaintances keep calling for frequent updates. Later, if the patient relapses, this same cycle starts all over again.

• **To conserve energy, some families find it helps to mail periodic form letters to keep friends and loved ones updated.** This doesn't have to be the job of a directly involved family member;

ask someone else to handle the news reporting. Choose someone who likes to write letters—a person in the circle who typically sends holiday cards, remembers birthdays, etc.

- **Another helpful tool is the "telephone tree"** where the family speaks directly to only a few select people, who then branch out to phone others.

We found out about J.'s cancer just before Thanksgiving. I just couldn't imagine writing holiday cards with this kind of news! Someone I know gave me a handout on holidays and grief, and it said to send out a form letter before the holidays. This would free you up to avoid writing cards completely, if you wanted. I felt a little strange about doing it, but it really did turn out to be a good idea because we got all kinds of wonderful cards and calls and even a few unexpected presents. I wrote back when I felt like it, but I didn't feel guilty about not "reaching out" during the holidays—I figured I'd given everyone a pretty understandable excuse!

In fact, the following spring, I got a phone call from a longtime friend I only write at Christmas and on her birthday. She said she had really appreciated the form letter, but how was J. doing now? She said she'd been worried for months but she'd been afraid to call. And she encouraged me to send out another form letter to give an update on J.'s prognosis, so other people wouldn't have to worry and wonder.

- **Sometimes, it's easiest to set up a policy of "no news is good news."** Make your updates event driven, rather than calendar driven.

- **Recipients of such indirect or sporadic methods will appreciate the information,** regardless the messenger or the form it takes, and respect the fact that family members become exhausted by having to tell the story personally, scores of times.

- **These methods also enable patients and their loved ones to concentrate on things** *other* **than the physical illness** when they talk to their friends. Maybe they'd like to talk about anything *but* their situation, like gardening or politics or college basketball. Helpful friends learn to follow their lead, and let the family member guide the conversation.

NOTES

5

BAD DAYS

- **Any person on this voyage—either a patient or loved one—can expect to have bad days.** Emotions may shut down, anger may explode, simple tasks seem pointless or impossible, tears won't come, tears won't stop, lethargy or distraction sets in. Sometimes these days are full of angry passion. Other times, the world seems empty, flat—there is barely enough energy to breathe.

- Our emotions and reactions—or lack of them—sometimes surprise us even more than they surprise others. When this happens, our most helpful friends look us straight in the eye to state firmly, **"You are *not* going crazy. You are *not* sinking."**

- **Bad days arrive *throughout* the process.** They do not go away as we grow more accustomed to this journey; they just change with the passing scenery.

A few years ago, after my dad had been sick for several years, an unbelievable thing happened. I actually got two tickets to the Super Bowl. Good tickets, too—nearly on the 50-yard line. My best friend and I got all settled into our seats and the opening hoopla began. All of a sudden, I felt this rush come over me and I started to bawl. I was thinking about Dad, and all the Super Bowls we'd watched on TV, dreaming how great it would be to see it live one day. And now I was actually there, in person, and he was the one who should have been next to me. But I couldn't even tell him about this—he has Alzheimer's and he doesn't know me anymore. So here I am, this grown man, sitting on the 50-yard line at the Super Bowl bawling my eyes out. And I'm not one of those quiche-eater guys who cries at the drop of a hat. I could feel people around me looking and wondering— "What's with this guy?!?" I was mortified. But I just couldn't make myself stop sobbing. And it took me totally by surprise.

- **Other people sometimes don't know what to do with us when we are having our bad days.** They say silly things like, "You have to pull yourself together." But why? To make *them* more comfortable? Remember, we are not about to drown, even if the people who love us imply that we are.

- **"Bad" days are actually good days,** as the mind and body work to protect and prepare us. We shut down. We emote. We wallow in melancholy and think about the past, present, and future. Eventually, we find perspective and peace. We are healing—taking this time for ourselves is *helpful* to us.

- **We must avoid feeling apologetic about our bad days.** Instead, we ought to celebrate them. They are doing us a world of good. Rather than calling them bad days we ought to **call them healing days.**

- **Helpful friends understand that only *we* can make the rules about our healing days.** No one else is able to tell us how to feel and act. And while well-intentioned friends may have creative ideas for how to "snap out of this" it is up to us to decide how to best spend our time—even if that means sitting alone in a dark room, or listening to sad music until we're sobbing, or other behaviors that those around us view as strange or morose.

"We've always had this family ritual," the wife of a cancer patient confided. "We play music every morning while we get ready for work and school. One morning, my husband put on Linda Ronstadt and Aaron Neville. Well, that lasted about five minutes! 'Cry like a rainstorm' was exactly what I started to do. I changed the music, but it was too late. Everything just crumpled around me.

"I told my husband I knew I wouldn't be in good shape that day—it felt like too much of a struggle to try to pull myself together. I didn't really want to feel better. I just felt like feeling bad. So, I stayed in bed all day. I took about three naps and cried the rest of the time in between.

"Luckily, my husband knew to leave me alone. Oh, he checked on me every once in a while, but he didn't complicate things by fussing over me. And he never made me feel guilty for giving myself a pity party, even though he's the one who's sick! He just trusted me to take care of myself. In a day or two I was lots better. Even pretty refreshed."

- **There are few things more depressing than being with someone who insists on cheering you up.** It adds unnecessary pressure. Explain this to anyone who tells you to "buck up." Kindly ask them to leave you alone until you have moved through the storm. And **avoid these people when the next healing day arrives.**

- Healing days are just one tool—mostly unconscious—we use to keep emotional balance. When we feel a bad day coming on, we can either try to squelch it or indulge it. When possible, try to pick the place and limit the damage. **It helps to remember we can control our healing days, rather than allowing them to control us.**

- **We need to give ourselves permission to be self-indulgent when these days arrive. It is equally important to pay close attention.** Make a conscious note of your specific feelings and physical reactions. Think about what you're doing to cope—try to discover what seems to help and what doesn't. We need to move our self-indulgence beyond mere pampering; we gain wisdom when we can use these times to collect information about which methods to use when the next healing day arrives.

- **Try to view these peaks and valleys of passion as one of the gifts of the experience.** There are not many moments in life when we can expect to feel things so profoundly, even if that feeling is profound emptiness. If possible, try to take the perspective of being fascinated by these emotions and reactions, even the scary, sad, and futile ones. Pay attention. Because, remember . . .

- **We *won't* always feel this way.**

NOTES

6

POSTURING

- **Most people with incurable illness hope that dignity and grace will be the hallmarks of their journey.** "If I have to do this," they say, "at least let me do it *well*." But being graceful and dignified all the time is exhausting, if not impossible.

- Therefore, it makes sense that **the person we present to the world is not the same person we present to our closest loved ones.** The patient's spouse may hear his partner described time and time again, by their mutual family and friends, as "marvelous, so strong, so optimistic!" At home, he sees a more multifaceted picture, and it isn't always pretty.

Everyone's always telling me how great she is, how together she is, how funny. And it's true, that's what she shows to the rest of the world. But I'm the one who finds her sobbing on the couch downstairs. I'm the one who sees her examining herself for new lesions. I'm the one who hears her ranting and raving. But if I ever told anybody these things, she'd kill me. Besides, no one would believe me. She's so different when she's with other people.

- **Patients and loved ones frequently speak of the posture, or "spin," they feel they must put on their situation.**

- **There are lots of reasons why we pose.** We hate the idea of others worrying about us, we don't care to be the center of attention, it's more efficient and publicly comfortable to deny the problem. Generally, we posture because it's the easiest way to deal with those people who are so busily dealing with *us*.

- **Often, we posture with outsiders** but have a few trusted insiders to whom we show our real feelings. **Sometimes, we posture with our inner circle most of all.** We feel we must protect them, or be strong for them, so we choose not to share our fears and negative feelings, sometimes even deciding to hide the truth.

- When returning to work, school, and other social activities, most patients in remission want to reenter their routines as quickly as possible, with little fanfare. But research finds they are still set apart from others—sometimes for six to twelve months and even longer. Psychologists call this the Lazarus syndrome. The patient is regarded as "special," a "hero," a "victim," more "vulnerable," even though he would most like to be regarded just like everybody else. **These reactions from others can cause a family to hide information** when they are dealing with employers, teachers, neighbors, or others, for fear of financial, social, or professional repercussions.

- **Worries about job security and social standing are often legitimate.** Tragically, the National Cancer Institute states that *one million* cancer patients report on-the-job discrimination. A disease like AIDS carries an even greater stigma; we don't have to go too far back in time to remember a boy named Ryan White. **It is essential that families on this journey know their rights** as employees, as insured persons, as members of their public school systems, as citizens of their state and federal governments.

We were very open about my situation when I was first diagnosed. We told everyone we know and love. But when I relapsed, I didn't want to tell my closest family and friends. I do talk about it, and I do get a lot of support, but I find myself turning more to acquaintances and work friends—I talk to people who aren't connected to me. Somehow when push came to shove, it was too hard to talk about it with the people who love me the very most. My own mother still doesn't know. She thinks I'm still in remission. And that's okay. It's easier this way.

- **Helpful friends avoid challenging the family's well-considered decisions to keep this situation private.** And they *never* disclose information to anyone else without the family's knowledge and permission.

- **Often, people in a primary relationship differ in their definitions of appropriate posturing.** They do not always see eye to eye about which people should get the complete truth, or when, how, or why. **This can be a major source of disagreements!** For instance, a wife hears her husband talking long-distance to her parents as if a cure is imminent. He hangs up, she attacks him. "Why didn't you tell them the *TRUTH*?" she asks. "You don't need to protect them! They're *MY* parents, anyhow!!"

- **It might seem most fair that the *patient* would get to call the shots about who gets what information. But this can be a gross oversimplification** and cause major conflicts. For instance, a husband argues with his incurably ill wife, "Fine, don't tell the kids. That will make this easier for you. But what about *me,* when I have to explain why we kept this from them, and you're not around to help me!?! We have to tell them. Together."

- **Things also get tricky because different people have vastly different needs for sharing their stories.** There is a possible gender difference here (for additional insight see Deborah Tannen, *You Just Don't Understand*). Many happily married couples experience arguments like this one: One partner, often the husband, says, "I don't want you sharing our personal problems with the whole wide world! Why do you insist on airing our dirty laundry in front of the whole neighborhood!" The other partner, often the wife, replies, "What makes you so afraid to ask for support? These are our friends! They love us and want to help!"

- **Ground rules can be established to share the true information about your family's situation.** It is also important for families to remember that *each* person has a valid perspective about posturing. (For help with these discussions, see Managing Family Conflict, p. 119.)

- **The ideal situation is when family members allow one another as much freedom and flexibility as possible** and encourage one another to tell their stories in whatever way they wish, to whomever they wish, without constraints.

- **When it comes to telling the story and sharing confidences, a patient's loved ones often experience serious struggles with guilt.** For instance, a spouse feels better after unloading her troubles to her best friend, but she feels guilty because she knows she's probably said more than the patient would want her to say. When the patient later asks, "How was your lunch with Nancy?" she casually replies, "Oh, fine, just the usual." Then she feels guilty for lying.

- **Loved ones can also be reluctant to share negatives with others because they somehow feel responsible for the patient's wellness.** The private mind-set runs like this: "Her attitude is so great, her treatment is going well. . . . If anything stands in the way of her getting better, it will be me— *my* fears, *my* irritations, *my* stamina."

He is so uncomplaining, and extremely hopeful. And he's doing really well right now. So whenever I worry or think about what could happen, it feels like a jinx! I start feeling guilty. They say that mind and body are really powerful, that people can will themselves sick and well sometimes. I believe that about the patient. But what about the people closest to a patient? If I allow myself to think about all the terrible things that could happen, do I create "bad karma" or negative energy? Do I cancel out the healing benefits of his attitude? Maybe it seems silly, but I really wonder and worry about that sometimes.

- **Obviously, loved ones don't have this kind of control over the situation;** wouldn't it be fabulous if they did?! How easy this journey would be, if only we could cure our loved ones by simple positive thinking.

- **It also seems wrong—or at least confusing—to want to complain about an ill loved one just at the time when he or she is being mentally and physically pushed to the limit.** We might feel selfish or ungrateful or unworthy. How can we gripe about our mate's irritability or insecurity, when he is enduring almost unbearable treatments and presenting a completely different (and far braver) picture to the rest of the world? It feels like a betrayal to tell the other side of the story.

- **This feeling of being wrong or selfish is reinforced time and time again for the grumbling family member,** because far too many well-meaning people respond with wide eyes and judgment when they hear a loved one complain about the patient. "Oh, but she's so *brave*!" they say. Or, "But just *imagine* what he's going through. . . . He's an absolute inspiration!" Obviously, the loved ones do see the bravery. And they can certainly do more than imagine what the patient is going through, because they are living with it, every single day. Helpful friends remind themselves that these closest loved ones also see lots of other things that outsiders don't.

- **We provide most help to a patient's loved ones when we let *them* talk—and even vent—about the patient,** rather than informing them of *our* thoughts about the patient. (See Listening and Responding with All Our Senses, p. 91.)

- **Those loved ones who are successful at seeing beyond our posturing are the ones who say, "Tell me more."** Sadly, too many loved ones hear the family express fears or negative feelings and instead say, "Oh, you can't really mean that!" Or even worse, "Oh, you *mustn't* say that!" These well-meaning friends believe they are helping us focus on the positives. In reality, they only cause us to hide our true feelings.

- **Our finest friends also help by accepting our posturing (even when they *can* see beneath it).** When we boast that we're gliding through this experience, it doesn't always help to be reminded how much we appear to be struggling to keep our heads above water. Close friends are truthful with us, yes. But they also use impeccable tact and timing.

- **Remember, posturing is not necessarily harmful,** even if it restricts completely honest expression. In fact, it can even help.

  - **Posturing probably contributes to wellness.** Since research indicates that attitude and physical state are so closely related, it makes sense that a person focusing on the positive may indeed feel better and experience a longer symptom-free survival.

  - **Posturing can be extremely efficient.** The patient and loved ones have many onlookers who are concerned and worried—which is wonderful and comforting but also time-consuming. Saying that "things are just fine" gets people off our backs (at least temporarily) when we prefer to focus our energies elsewhere.

  - **Posturing is tactful.** In every person's life, there are people who feel closer to you than you feel to them; they may call for frequent updates, but you really prefer not to deepen the relationship by sharing details. Posturing is an effective tool to stave off these people.

  - **Posturing builds a beautiful legacy** of how the patient and loved ones move through this experience.

- **In short, posturing is one of the family's more helpful coping mechanisms.** They just need to take care that they don't use it *exclusively*.

NOTES

7

COMMUNICATING WITH
THE MEDICAL TEAM

You know things are serious when your doctor tells you to "go home and have a few glasses of wine." Or when he asks you if you believe in a higher power. Maybe those sound like strange things for a doctor to say, but mine did. And I really appreciated it. He talks to me like I'm a whole person, not just a science project. He isn't afraid to bring up topics like spirituality, or how my kids are, or what future plans my family is making. We talk about lots of things, not just my symptoms and test results.

He treats me like a human being, and he cares about my whole family, not just my physical body. And that's good, because I care about so much more than just my physical body, these days. After all, my body has sort of given up on me, hasn't it! But my family hasn't. And my spirit hasn't. And thank goodness, neither has my doctor.

• **When a family is dealing with incurable illness, they soon find they're involved with *lots* of medical experts,** each with different advice and style. Some of these experts have compassion, some have clarity. The best medical professionals use both when they communicate.

• **Working with a *team* of medical experts can be confusing, especially in the beginning.** A patient who has never been seriously ill probably hasn't heard herself discussed by three different physicians, all crammed into the same examining room. Suddenly, the patient is seen by a referring physician, various specialists in the specific disease, separate specialists in the treatment, and any other colleague these experts want him to see. The team begins to build itself, as experts pull in other experts: occupational therapists, home-care nurses, social workers, and more.

- **All this attention is wonderful, and also a little scary.** While it is comforting to know that so many experts are pulling for the patient, this attention also underscores the seriousness of the situation. Because so many people are seeing the patient, it is helpful for the patient and family to **specify who is on the medical team and who is there in a full-time capacity.** The patient can get clarification merely by asking each expert: "Just what is *your* role in my case? How involved will *you* be?"

- **With a given team member, it can be extremely helpful to briefly re-cap, without monopolizing the appointment time, what has transpired in recent consultations with *other* team members.** "I'll start by spending just a minute or two telling you what Dr. H. said in my last visit" is a wise beginning to any meeting with a new team member. This helps ensure that people are on the same wavelength and also proves efficient — the physician doesn't waste time informing the family of issues other team members have already covered.

- **It helps to mutually decide on a captain,** a specific physician who is the family's first contact when any questions or concerns arise. In a sense, the captain is at the helm, supervising the case. He or she keeps close contact with the family and also helps coordinate information flowing among various team members. **The captain might change, during the course of an illness.** For instance, with a leukemia patient, the first captain might be a referring hematologist. Later, the captain might be a specialist in chemotherapy. Once the patient completes treatment, the captain becomes an oncologist, and so forth.

- **It is *not* necessary for the captain to be the one with the most expertise about a particular disease.** Team members are already continuously consulting about the situation behind the scenes; through other less directly involved members, the captain has access to any expertise needed.

- **It *is* crucial that the team captain be compassionate.** The family truly needs to *like* and *trust* this individual.

I like my doctors, for the most part. But there's one who takes herself so seriously. My family gets by on humor, so we laugh and joke with the rest of the team, a lot! It helps. But every time I make a wisecrack to her, she always seems to look at me like, "Grow up, will you? This is life and death stuff!" She never once cracks a smile. I always feel like telling her, "Hey, lighten up a little. I'm the one who's dying here, not you!"

- **Since team members will be *interacting among themselves,* it is important the family feels they do so effectively.** Are team members clear on each other's perspectives? Do they write up their reports and memos in a timely manner? Are they efficient and effective in their ability to share information with one another? Do they ever complain about being confused by actions taken by other members? Do they ever misplace the patient's medical file? Do they ever bad-mouth each other? If so, speak to team members directly about these concerns.

- **People with serious or rare ailments do run the risk of encountering a few prima donna personalities,** though this is probably less typical than we might think. And who cares, so long as this person has the expertise the family needs! Just keep the prima donna in an advisory role, choose someone else as the family's team captain, and communicate more directly with the medical experts the family likes.

- **If we don't want a particular person on our medical team, we need to say so. We aren't obligated to supply a good reason, and we aren't expected to justify our feelings to anybody.** We can—and *should*—make such a decision if we are concerned about the person's medical competence. But we can also just as easily eliminate a team member because of personality issues.

Health care workers should not take this personally; such changes happen all the time. **Sometimes, the medical team insists that we keep a member we don't like—for expertise or for insurance reasons. If so, we can respect the team's judgment but still minimize contact.** Just say, "If you think Dr. X. is essential because of his expertise, I'll agree. But I'd prefer to have the *other* doctors examine me."

• **Sometimes, one family member might have a problem with a particular team member's behavior or attitude, but other loved ones aren't bothered.** For instance, the wife says to her ill husband, "I know *you* like him and trust him, but when he talks to me he seems very condescending." **It is important to consider the feelings of *all* closely connected family members and their opinions of the medical team.** This is a situation that affects much more than the patient. Close family members need to feel comfortable with the medical team, too.

One of my doctors was so pompous. He drove me crazy. He never looked me in the eye, he spoke a million miles a minute, and in my few appointments with him, he always seemed like he was too busy, or on his way somewhere else. Funny, though, my husband really liked him. He said, "He's the smartest one of the bunch." And it's true, he did write up a very thorough report after my first visit with him. He knew his stuff, I'll give him that. But I hated having to talk to him. So whenever I could, I let my husband do the talking. That doctor probably thought I was a real wimp. But the truth was, I just didn't care to deal with him.

• **When commenting on communication difficulties, it helps to be specific.** Rather than saying, "You just don't explain things so I can understand them," try, "When I ask questions, the answers are very fast, with lots of 'buzzwords' and it is hard for me to digest everything." **A specific observation will help the medical expert correct the problem.** In this last example, the physician or nurse now knows two specific changes to make: slow down and use more common vocabulary. But if a complaint is broad and vague ("You can't seem to explain things!") the medical expert will be scratching her head, wondering what to do differently.

- **Sometimes we're tempted to replace team members who use "medicalese," those frustrating people who seem incapable of explaining our situation in words *we* can understand.** It's easy to take this phenomenon personally, or even accuse the offending doctor of being on a "power trip." But this communication breakdown isn't really about power—it's just a job hazard like any other. Try asking a carpenter to explain deck construction, or a banker to explain refinancing. *Any* professional speaks with a highly specialized vocabulary, and it's common for experts in *any* area to forget that the layperson doesn't understand.

- **Rather than getting frustrated by doctorese, it's better to try asking the expert for the information again, in a different way.** Say, "Could you explain that again, only using different words?" or "Could you say that again, please, except much more slowly?" **When we still feel unclear, we specifically instruct the doctor *not* to explain again. Instead, we ask to repeat what we think we heard, *then* get clarification.** (Otherwise, the physician continues to try to explain, gets even more frustrated, and makes things even less intelligible.) Interrupt a third attempt to explain by saying, "I'm starting to get it, and just to be sure, let me say back to you what I *think* you mean, and then you correct me where I'm unclear, okay?"

- **Patients and their loved ones can educate themselves in the language of their specific illness.** A good dictionary is invaluable; an expensive medical dictionary is not mandatory. You might be able to borrow one from a friend or relative; otherwise, any thorough, unabridged dictionary will do the trick, especially in the early stages of information seeking (that's where my family learned the meaning of *alopecia,* which means hair loss, though we still probably aren't pronouncing it correctly).

• **Patients and loved ones can also ask medical team members to define terms, of course, but the more homework the family does, the better.** After all, why waste valuable consulting time going over definitions that are easily accessible from other sources? Further, we need to *discourage* the medical team from using this kind of language with us; clarity improves when they can put their thoughts and suggestions into *layperson's* terms. Just ask them to repeat what they have said in different (not medical) words.

• The first few times you read a medical file—or during the first few attempts at comprehending medical journal articles about the patient's illness—you will encounter *scores* of new terms. Take heart! **This new vocabulary can be learned surprising quickly, because the same terms are used time and time again.**

• **It helps to highlight new terms as you encounter them, then create a glossary on a separate piece of paper** to avoid looking up the same word twice. Keep the glossary handy at all times and make copies for other loved ones. After a short time, family and friends won't even need to refer to the glossary very often. As my father used to say, **"Use a word three times and it's yours."**

• **Patients and their loved ones approach the medical team with different levels of information and knowledge.** Some of us are info starved while others already feel overwhelmed. **Give the info hounds the jobs of researching the illness and options.** (A fast, effective method for performing such research appears in the Appendix. See Researching the Illness and Options, p. 207.)

• **Sometimes, the medical team seems to discourage us from using our new vocabulary—or they grow edgy when we talk about our *own* research about our illness.** They may be nervous we'll have misunderstandings of the technical jargon, or they fear we'll draw incorrect conclusions. They operate on the principle "A little knowledge can be a dangerous thing." This is valid! Appreciate and directly acknowledge their years of training and experience. Ask for their assistance in interpreting the information, rather than using the information to challenge what they say.

- **Patients and loved ones need to steel themselves for the information they uncover. It is essential first to determine just how much they want to research and know.** For example, if only five percent of all patients with a specific disease live twenty-four months, we're likely to find out—in black and white. This research wasn't written for patients; it was usually written for professional caregivers. The information is objective, graphic, and to the point. **It isn't as though we can forget the statistics and the photographs once we've seen them.**

- **It would be easier if there were clear-cut methods for dealing with incurable illness. There aren't.** That's why some diseases are called incurable in the first place; the precise recipe for success has yet to be discovered. Patients and loved ones enhance the relationship they have with their medical experts once they can accept this. The more comfortable a person becomes with ambiguity, the better. We need to avoid getting sidetracked by things we cannot control. **We *cannot* expect our medical experts to provide answers and assurances they don't have.**

- **It helps to be prepared that medical team experts might *disagree* with each other, perhaps even passionately, about some facets of the patient's diagnosis and treatment.** These differences of opinion can be disconcerting and confusing; they are also valuable.

My doctors were pretty vocal, and they didn't completely agree on what I should do. Maybe that would have made it easier, but it was okay just to listen to them and get as many ideas as possible. And it was interesting to try to figure out why they all believed what they did. It was pretty simple, really. The cardiologist was worried about my heart. The ENT guy was concerned with the tumor in my throat. The radiologist kept pushing for radiology, and a different oncologist pushed for chemo. We all came together in the end, but it was easy to see how each doctor would focus on what he knew best.

- **Avoid feeling frightened if the medical team says they don't know something,** or if they say they need to do more research. This is normal, especially with rare or complicated cases. In general, it is unlikely that all members of the medical team are completely familiar with the very latest research—at least not immediately. **This is an issue of *statistics,* not competence!** Physicians are expected to keep current on a massive array of new information, with research being published even as you read this (thank goodness). It makes sense that a physician might have only *skimmed* articles on a specific illness, especially if she has encountered that illness only a few times during her entire career.

- **And with rare disorders often *no one* knows,** even those who *are* current in the research. Plain and simple, there haven't been enough cases studied, and the medical team cannot be definitive in answering the family's questions and concerns. **This is frustrating. But it isn't anybody's *fault.***

- **Patients and their loved ones are advised to take as much responsibility for researching the illness as they possibly can, and the effective medical team encourages any efforts at patient/family education.** In fact, since there are often no clear-cut answers to an incurable illness, the team will appreciate a family's efforts to understand the factors that go into recommendations. For instance, there might be some cases where the treatment could turn out to be worse than the disease itself. **Doctors need the family to be aware of the risks and ramifications of their decisions.**

- **The more we know about our own situation, the wiser our voice in the decisions that affect us, but with such knowledge also comes responsibility.** We need to decide just how much stamina and energy we'll have for researching this illness and its treatment options.

- **Patients and their loved ones need to place their trust in their medical experts.** We scoff they are not "godlike." Yet in subtle ways, we do expect them to perform some rather godlike functions. We expect them to encourage us, to help us gather and decipher new information and insights, to guide us in making life-changing decisions. We expect them to be wise, impartial, to set forth the right decision with compassionate clarity—all while insisting they should recall the unique signatures of every specific patient's situation. Sometimes we even expect them to cure us. These are big demands even for most real gods.

Dr. Holms set that first family appointment for after hours, so we wouldn't get interrupted. We were there from 5:30 to 7:30, right through his dinner hour. He would have stayed there even longer if we needed to talk more.

A few days later I was thinking about that . . . his level of commitment, how caring he was. I thought about all the other dinners he's probably missed. Being an oncologist, he works with lots of "incurable" cases like ours.

I wrote him a thank-you note. I sent a copy to his boss and the hospital's board of directors. But the people I wanted to thank even more were his family. I want his wife and kids to know what a difference he made. I want them to understand what he's doing, those times he doesn't show up at a school play or soccer game. He's helping some family find peace and perspective, while they try to deal with the scariest news of their lives. I want his family to know, we really needed him that night, and he came through for us. No matter what eventually happens to my daughter, I'll never forget what he did for us.

NOTES

8

FAMILIES FACING
ILLNESS

· **A family is where we find it.** For many patients, their birth certificates or adoption papers are not a defining factor.

For twelve years, I've lived with my best friend and her daughter. My parents are back east—I moved to Oregon when I was in college, got married, bought a house when I was twenty-four. Christine and I were both divorced about the same time, and she moved into my house when Allison was only two. When I got cancer, my mother panicked. She spent months pressuring me to move back home. She said, "You have to come home. You don't have any family out there to help you."

At first, I got sucked into believing her. I almost moved back to Philadelphia. I guess I had this Ozzie and Harriet idea of what a family is "supposed" to be. But Christine and Allison were really hurt that I would even consider it. They were right; they've felt like my family for a lot longer than my "real" family ever did. This is where I belong.

· **Blood is *not* always thicker than water.** Biology and legal sanctions have never been a necessary requirement for family membership. A group of friends is one patient's family. The family of another is her lesbian partner, though years ago they perhaps publicly posed as spinster friends or cousins. A foster family feels like home to still a third. The *patient* determines who is family, not genetics or law. **Our truest friends accept our family, however *we* define it.**

- **Research shows that symptom-free survival is more likely when family is present—regardless the biology or legality of the relationship.** In general, patients' families often say their personal relationships are unaffected and even *enhanced* by the experiences of living with incurable illness. We families who live with serious illness find we become wiser or more loving and more appreciative of each other.

- **At the same time, these essential people in our lives are also the ones who can cause us our biggest frustrations. We are hardest on those we love most deeply.** We make more demands on them, trusting them not to abandon us, even if we aren't polite or kind. Our families drive us crazy sometimes. But when one of our members is incurably ill, we are generally fortunate to have one another.

- **Sociologists often liken the family to a mobile—members hang from the individual strings, continuously gyrating, connected but still separate.** When life's turbulence occurs, our mobile swings and members may even collide and become tangled, but eventually the mobile—or family system—is able to right itself. However, when the family experiences incurable illness or the death of a member, that member's piece of the mobile is changed beyond compare—perhaps even cut off from the mobile completely. The family now has to shift around, maybe even add new items, before it can find balance again. The original mobile is permanently altered; it can never be like it was before. **Helpful friends appreciate this adjustment process. They remember that achieving family balance takes time, skill, and considerable patience. And sometimes, they even gently remind us of this fact.**

- **Each family member brings a unique perspective to this experience; each has a unique relationship with the incurable person.** A man's illness is much different for his children than for his spouse. His parents bring other perspectives, his siblings still others. The list expands to best friends, close friends, acquaintances, peers, and anyone else who has a history of interacting with him.

- **Personality preferences play a part.** One man is happiest when the kitchen table is encircled by friends and loved ones. His spouse, on the other hand, needs solitude to "restore the batteries"—she just wants everyone to pack up and go home. Or perhaps one person is quickly decisive: "Let's get this show on the road—remember what the doctor said, the longer we wait, the faster it will spread." But the other needs to gather more information and wants to postpone treatment choices until the last possible moment: "Don't be so impulsive. The doctor *also* said we still have time, and we'll make a better decision if we get a third and fourth opinion." (For more insight, see Keirsey and Bates, *Please Understand Me.*)

- **We frequently seek out mates who *complement* our personalities rather than match them.** Yes, opposites *do* attract—the benefit is that we can each tone down and simultaneously bring out the best in the other. But our opposing styles and personalities can also be frustrating and even infuriating. Each family member wants to arrive at the same destination, yet they get there by entirely different tributaries. And we sometimes spend too much energy arguing over who has a better sense of direction. **Helpful friends and loved ones gently remind us that no way is the right way—there are just *different* ways.**

- **Families also have distinct personalities and styles of interacting.** Some families are soft-spoken, some are profane, some shout, some sing, some are sarcastic. Just because a family is very loud and argumentative doesn't mean they are unhappy or ready to separate. Just because a family is quite reserved and physically unaffectionate doesn't mean they are uncaring or stuffing their true feelings.

I was a hospice volunteer for a family that spent lots of time "maintaining" their household. They wanted me to wash windows, clean cupboards—I did stuff for them that I haven't done in my own house in years. They never seemed to spend much time talking or sharing. At first I thought, how sad, here they are just making work, trying to avoid the bigger issue. But then I realized, hey, they were coping, and well. Overall, they did a really good job taking care of each other. They just did it differently than I would have.

- **Friends and loved ones help most when they observe the family's rules and communication styles and abide by them.** Our best friends avoid interrupting our family's patterns, *even when they disagree with them.* For instance, now is not the time to convince your best friend's husband he's a sexist pig; now isn't the time to pressure a teenager to talk more.

- **It can be very helpful for families to schedule a weekly face-to-face meeting, to discuss changes in the situation, new medications, scheduling, and so on.** People in the primary caregiving circle should make every effort to attend, or phone someone for new information immediately afterward—this alleviates confusion and spreads the caregiving responsibilities more fully.

- **The day-to-day irritations of life don't stop when a person has an incurable illness.** Kids continue to have trouble at school, cars still break down, basements still get flooded. These daily stresses just compound the bigger pressure. **Families also have major problems,** such as financial troubles, chemical dependency, damaged relationships. The functional problems that existed in this family prior to the illness are still there and may even be exacerbated.

- **Friends and loved ones can help by taking the initiative to handle some of the minor day-to-day hassles found in *any* family**—by loaning a car because the family's car is in the shop, by driving a daughter to get her cavities filled, by fixing the lawn mower without being asked, by chipping the ice off the sidewalk.

- **Friends do *not* help, however, when they try to fix a family's major issues.** It is a big mistake to think a family's deep-seated problems can be easily solved, especially during such a traumatic time. For example, deathbed reconciliations do occur, but romantic illusions are best left at the theater.

- **It is equally important for friends to be wary of entanglement.** These primary loved ones push and pull against each other, just like the mobile. We need to avoid getting trapped between spouses, between siblings, between parents and children, etc.

- **And family members mustn't give in to the temptation to gang up on each other.** We mustn't exclude family members whose behaviors, personalities, and communication styles we find difficult.

- **Finally, strong families and their finest friends are always mindful of this important fact**—there isn't a family in the world that is perfectly functional . . . or functionally perfect.

NOTES

9

TALKING WITH KIDS
ABOUT ILLNESS AND DYING

We were at a restaurant with my mother and her friends. My son, who is nine, started complaining because there was a tomato slice on his hamburger. My mother said, "Oh, c'mon, Scott, you can handle this." Scott started to laugh, picked off the tomato, and then said rather brazenly, "You're right, Grandma—I can handle anything. I can even handle my parents dying." He was so cocky. My mother's reaction was a shocked and automatic "Oh no, Scott, you couldn't handle that!" And just as automatically, even with a touch of anger, I said, "Oh yes, he can. It would be hard, but even that Scott can handle."

I guess I felt a little angry with my mother because for two years, ever since my first relapse, Scott and I have had these kinds of conversations. And the fact is, he probably will have to handle it—he already is handling it—much sooner than most kids. I want him to be as prepared and confident as possible. I'm not about to let anyone—even my own mother—undermine him. You know, people don't talk with kids about this because they say, "Kids don't understand, they can't deal with it." If that's true, it's only because we haven't included them.

- **People make a huge mistake when they try to shield children from serious illness and dying.** It is essential to be truthful and straightforward with them. **We *don't* help by bombarding children with lots of information at once. Instead, provide insights in bits and pieces,** as events unfold. Be guided by the knowledge that we always can add more later. But also remember, kids can handle much more information than most people think.

- **Many people assume children will somehow let us know when they want to talk.** They say, "I'll talk to her whenever she asks. Whatever she wants to know, I'll tell her the truth." Unfortunately, many children have questions and concerns that are never voiced; they can *sense* that adults are uncomfortable and they become reticent about initiating a discussion. **Begin the conversation for them, rather than waiting.** Just say, "I'd like to talk a bit about my illness, okay?" Or, "I'll bet there are a few questions about all these treatments Mom is getting."

- **Children have two very different perspectives of a serious illness, particularly when the illness is their own.** They have a medical perspective, and they have a meanings perspective.

- **The medical perspective is often highly accurate in terms of its vocabulary or clinical descriptions of treatment.** Even a five-year-old might say, "I have cancer, but really it's called leukemia. I had two biopsies, and the doctors gave me chemotherapy." These words coming from such tiny little lips might surprise and even inspire friends and loved ones. They make us believe the child is self-confident and strong, coping well.

- **Don't be fooled—the medical perspective is *not* an accurate reflection of the child's true understanding of the situation.** The astute child is mostly mimicking the words of the adults around her. Many children with big vocabularies are living with sad and scary misconceptions about the *meanings* of their situation. For instance, that precocious little five-year-old might add "Leukemia means my cancer is in my blood. My blood got bad because of the time I fell on my bike and didn't tell. I got infected, because I was too afraid to let Mommy clean out my cut."

- **Helpful people listen *beyond* the child's medical descriptions. They ask questions to uncover the child's true feelings on the meaning of the situation.** For example, "You sure have been through a lot. What's it like?" Or, "I wonder what the doctors are trying to find out by doing all these tests?" Through such questions you can start a dialogue, and you will be able to determine the child's misconceptions. Then, you can slowly begin to address them.

- **Avoid addressing each misconception as it occurs, one by one.** For instance, many loving adults mistakenly begin by *informing* the child, "Oh no, it wasn't the bike accident that caused this!" then launch into a lecture about leukemia. This immediate lecture prevents the adult from uncovering other misconceptions (for instance, the girl says she's bald because her hair is brown instead of red, like her brother's). A better initial response to the child's misconception is, "Tell me more about that bike accident. Where did you get cut?" Or, "Did you have to take any special medicine because of that cut?" **Listen to the child's *entire* perspective. Only then can you discover and slowly begin to address all the misconceptions.**

- **Children take what we say literally.** Be aware of metaphors used in their presence; for example, "The tumor has eaten away her lungs" could be confusing or even terrifying for a young child.

- **The content of a child's communication is often a shield for the emotional experience they are having,** particularly with adolescents. Kids say outlandish things, just for effect. For instance, a twelve-year-old says, "It's fair that Mom got cancer. I told her to quit smoking and she wouldn't listen. She *deserves* this." Instead of responding in shock and outrage, a helpful friend or loved one hears and responds to the *deeper* meanings, the feelings of anger, fear, loss of control, etc. For instance, we could say, "What did your mother say when you told her to quit?" Or, "It sounds like you've known about the dangers of smoking since you were young—I wonder why adults can't be so smart. What do *you* think?"

- **Helpful friends and loved ones *encourage* the expression of difficult feelings**—sadness, anger, disbelief, fear. This is especially important for teens, who likely already experience a strained communication with their parents. Adolescents are further affected because of peer pressure and their heightened body awareness. It's very difficult to be different—either because you have a very ill family member, or because you are very ill yourself.

- **School is a child's workplace.** An adult experiences isolation and feelings of being different when returning to work during serious illness; this phenomenon is heightened for children, who have less history with such situations and a limited repertoire of behaviors. Imagine being a fourteen-year-old boy who one day shows up at school without hair, or whose mother turns up at a school play, rail thin, in a wheelchair. It isn't easy.

- **Children need to be prepared to be snubbed by their class-mates, former friends, and sometimes even teachers.** Help them understand that not everyone will be capable of treating them like they did before—it's wise to directly acknowledge this. Tell a child, "It isn't that *you* are so different, it's just that *other* peo-ple feel awkward. They aren't sure what to say. They may seem to turn away from you, but it's probably only because they are scared of saying the wrong thing."

- **Others may seek out friendship with the child on false pre-tenses** because they are curious, because they feel pity, because it makes *them* feel special to know someone who is enduring so much. But when the novelty is over, so is the friendship. A child in this situation needs an extra dose of healthy human skepti-cism. Have a conversation about fair-weather friendships, share your own painful episodes about such friendships to normalize the child's experience, and gently suggest, "People are friends for different reasons and on lots of different levels. Some are deeper and stronger than others."

- **At the same time, let the child know the importance of taking the initiative,** of being the one who gives until a rela-tionship gets back on track and people become more comfort-able with the situation. Prepare the child for people who might adopt a hands-off attitude—or an overly solicitous one. Your forewarning will make the child's later pain easier to understand

and bear. Meanwhile, continue to shower love and acceptance at home.

My son's girlfriend was diagnosed with cancer last year—she was only a sophomore in high school. She missed three months of school, and going back was traumatic. She was bloated by the chemo, she had lost her hair, and she needed a wheelchair for the fatigue. The first few days my son said everyone made a big deal about having her back, but then people seemed to pull away from her. She wasn't included in the group, that kind of thing. One day she was standing at her locker and a couple of kids pushed her chair down the hall, saying, "You faker. You don't even need that thing." The next morning, my son told me she stood up during homeroom and said, "I have something to say. I don't have this wheelchair because I can't walk—I need it because I get tired from the chemotherapy they're using to treat my cancer. That's also why my face is fat and why I'm bald. One day, I'll look like I did before, I hope. I'm really the same person I was before the cancer, except that I've had some pretty amazing experiences in the past few months. I think I'm even a little smarter, even though I know I'm not much to look at right now. If anyone wants to talk about it, great. Otherwise, I hope you'll either treat me like you did before, or leave me alone."

- **Reentry into school life can be expedited when children are provided an opportunity to speak openly and publicly about these experiences. Empower children by showing them they can use their lives and experiences to educate others.** Perhaps your niece would like to explain amputation—using herself as a visual aid. Or maybe your son could tell his class what it's like to have hospice visitors in his home. Or a third grader you know could write an article for the school paper about being the friend of an AIDS patient.

- **Well-meaning school systems often need advice on how to handle these difficult situations in the classroom.** Certainly, teachers are no more comfortable with this topic than the rest of us. They need guidance and training, too. Some loving teachers make the mistake of putting a child on the spot without structure or warning. "Tommy, why don't you help us understand what has been happening in your family these past few months."

- **A better approach adopts an exercise used in support groups—each classmate writes down questions on index cards, anonymously. The cards are placed in a big bag or bowl. The child pulls out cards, one by one, answering each. This method puts the entire class in charge** of the discussion, rather than focusing predominantly on the child who is ill or living with serious family illness. The anonymity also encourages real questions, even the "scary" or "stupid" ones. For example, "Is your father going to die?" Or, "Is it hard to go to the bathroom without your leg?" **Family members can take the initiative to *suggest* this method to their children's schools.** Adults might wish to accompany a younger child to such a question-answer session, but most adolescents are more empowered if they handle this discussion alone. Whatever the choice, teachers and family members alike need to make sure it's the *child* doing the talking.

- **Children need straightforward information about their own illness. Parents often say their greatest anxiety was *before* telling an incurable child s/he might not live long.** They worried and fretted over how to conduct this painful discussion, but the actual conversation was often a poignant and peaceful surprise. Many people report their kids saying things like, "I already knew I was probably going to die before I grow up. I figured it out a long time ago, but I didn't want to say anything because I thought it would make *you* sad." Most people understand their circumstances even if the words haven't been uttered—kids included.

- **Sometimes kids catch us off guard before we're ready. They ask, right in the middle of Monopoly, "Is Mommy going to die?"** An honest response respects the child's intelligence and provides hope, pointing to the fact that life is full of unknowns.

"Well, we're *all* going to die, because every living thing does, and no one ever knows exactly when or how it will happen. This illness Mommy has is serious—and it could turn out her life will be shorter. But we're also very hopeful."

My daughter and I were at a restaurant when suddenly she blurted, totally out of nowhere, "Is Daddy going to die in two weeks?" I was so surprised I almost laughed out loud. Two weeks?!? I have no idea where she got two weeks. My husband looks great and he isn't anywhere close to dying. But I collected myself and said, "No, honey, Daddy isn't going to die in two weeks."

"Well, is he going to die in two months then?"

"Oh, no. Not at all. Daddy will be around for a long, long time."

"How long?"

I wanted to be truthful, so I said, "Well, we don't really know exactly. But I guess we could say there's a chance he might not be around when you're in high school." I waited, worried about her reaction.

"Oh," she said, and picked up a french fry, looking all happy. Then she went on to another topic. I sat there stunned. High school must sound like an eternity to a third grader, while to me, it's just a blink of my eye. She gave me a new perspective, that's for sure.

- **Kids want to know what death means, *physically*.** We need to explain with clarity precisely what happens to a human body when it expires. We can help by talking specifically about the heart, the breathing, the brain. We need to avoid confusing euphemisms like "sleeping eternally" or "passed on." It's essential for any child to understand that physical death is permanent.

- **Kids have *practical* concerns, too.** "Who will take care of me?" "Will we have to move?" "What if you *both* die?" "What if Daddy marries someone else and I don't like her?" It is the wise adult who addresses these concerns directly and calmly—without necessarily waiting for the child to bring up the topic (because this might never happen).

- **When talking with children about the afterlife and other spiritual issues, we need to be true to ourselves and our own beliefs. But we must also leave room for the child's interpretations** by acknowledging, "No one knows for sure, but I *can* tell you what *I* believe." Then, we remember to ask the child the most important question of all, "Now, you tell me, what do *you* believe?"

- **Heaven is a difficult concept for anyone, and perhaps even more confusing for a small child with a literalist perspective.** "What if heaven is too crowded and Mommy can't find a parking place?" "How can Grandma and Grandpa be in heaven at the same time when they're divorced?" And, "Who will be with Grandpa's *new* wife, when *she* dies?"

- **Many speak of heaven because we believe in it fervently and find the idea comforting, but wise people are also aware the concept can backfire if it isn't handled well.** For instance, telling a child, "Your uncle Bruce is in heaven watching over you" may bring peace *or* the feeling of being spied upon and vulnerable. Or, telling a child about her sibling, "Greta is such a good little girl, God just wants to bring her up to heaven a little earlier so He can be with her" might make the child worry, *But why doesn't God want me? Does He think I'm bad?* Or, this well-meaning remark could make the child choose to "be bad" on purpose, so as to avoid an untimely death.

- **Sadly, many kids whose loved ones are ill experience lots of unnecessary guilt concerning their role in it.** They may remember a time they shouted, "I hate you! I wish you would die!" and feel responsible. Or they recall a time their mother screamed, "You kids are driving me crazy!" Now she suffers dementia and they secretly think, "Gosh, I guess I really *did*!!" Again, a trusted adult helps by bringing up these issues and directly addressing them—without necessarily waiting for the child to do so.

- **Try not to be fearful of inviting even very small children to be in the presence of a loved one who is seriously ill.** We sometimes hesitate to expose children unless we have to—the nieces and nephews, the godchildren and grandkids. This can rob everyone of a significant and even positive experience.

- **We can prepare children to see even a days-from-death loved one by fully describing the person's appearance and abilities. It is wise to begin talking a day or two before the visit,** not so much warning that the child has time to grow anxious, but enough time for him to mentally get ready. In our first conversation, we spend about ten minutes making specific statements like these (but certainly not too many of them, and not necessarily in this order):

  - *"Aunt June is very sick, and we're thinking of visiting tomorrow afternoon. You are welcome to come with us. But you don't have to, either."*

  - *"She doesn't look the same as you remember. She has changed a lot. She's very thin and weak. Her face is very pale."*

  - *"She sleeps a lot; she might not want to talk to us while we're there."*

  - *"Her voice is different—she sounds raspy. Her breathing is very loud; sometimes it sounds scary."*

  - *"She loves you very much, and she's the same Aunt June inside—she just looks different. But she can hear and understand you, just like always."*

  - *"You can touch her if you want. But you don't have to, either."*

  - *"You can tell her you love her, if you want. Or you can decide to be quiet and say nothing at all, if you'd rather."*

  - *"You cannot catch Aunt June's sickness. She doesn't have any germs that could ever make any of us sick."*

- *"Seeing someone who is so sick is scary, even for lots of grown-ups. I'm afraid, too, sometimes. But we can be together the whole time, if you want."*

- *"If you decide you want some time alone with Aunt June, you can let me know that, too. I'll just step outside the room and you can close the door, but if you need me you can call me."*

- *"Whatever you decide about this visit is okay. And you can change your mind about any decision you make, at any time, even after we're already there."*

- **Phrases like these will likely elicit more questions from the child.** It's best to spend some time addressing such concerns, but take care to end the conversation before things become tense, "obsessive," or redundant. Throughout the next day, be prepared to talk calmly and spontaneously, as new questions or concerns arise.

- **We are wise to *expect* "acting out" from children who live with serious illness—whether the patient is a loved one or the child himself.** Kids in this situation sometimes repeat questions just to be "smart-alecks." They push every single elevator button at the twelve-story hospital where they take their treatments. They are insolent to the people who try to comfort them. They tell stupid knock-knock jokes to everyone in earshot—*loud.* Truly, they can be downright obnoxious. Obviously, it is important that children remain relatively respectful. **But they are also under tremendous pressure. Give kids a break about their behaviors at such a difficult time.**

- **Child development experts tell us that children experience fear and grief very differently than adults. Typically, their episodes with these complicated emotions are shorter, *but they are no less intense.*** If old enough to speak, a child is old enough to understand what's happening, at least on some level. We shortchange everyone involved if we fail to appreciate this.

- **Helpful friends and loved ones understand that children handle their emotions in highly individual ways—just like adults**

do. When coping with incurable illness, some kids will be quite loud, hyperactive, maybe angry, and highly verbal. Others will be pensive and seek solitude. Still others need lots of hugging and physical reassurance, almost to the point of clinging. **None of these ways is any better than another; they are just *different*.** It is a mistake to compare siblings' reactions; it's wrong to assume that one child is handling this experience better than another just because he or she is being more open about it or acting less angry or needy.

- *Expect* **children to play, even in sad or serious settings.** Don't be surprised, don't even raise an eyebrow, when one moment a boy is sobbing uncontrollably at his mother's bedside, then five minutes later he's running around outside with a good friend, screaming with joy and laughter.

- **Provide plenty of outlets for play**—for ill kids in a hospital or hospice setting, for healthy siblings, for children coping with change throughout this demanding journey.

  - *Physical play* **is essential for venting.** Give children clay, or hammer and nails, plant a garden with them, pound dough while baking bread, suggest a game of tag, build a tower and topple it, have a pillow fight, roughhouse with them, etc.

  - *Creative play* **is helpful for expressing.** Provide paper and markers so a child can draw. Write and sing songs together, make a scrapbook together, write poetry, give them a diary or a blank book journal. Many therapists find it helpful to have a child draw a before-the-illness and after-the-illness picture of daily life—or perhaps a before/after portrait of the patient—as a method of generating discussion and exploring issues.

  - *Imaginary play* **helps children make sense of events.** Don't be disturbed to find a child lying very still pretending to be dead; don't be overly concerned when he buries a stuffed animal. Observe these actions and use them for discussion openers if you care to, and you might even choose to participate in the "funeral." But *do not interfere* with a child's play even when it seems bizarre to you. Trust the child to know what's best.

- **Friendships *outside* the immediate family are important for any child, but especially for those who live with incurable illness.** These kids need to get away and "be normal" as often as possible. It is essential to make the extra effort to arrange playdates and social outings for these children, and their families are helped more than they can say when the initiative comes from a family that *isn't* coping with serious illness. **If your child is friendly with another child who lives with family illness, pick up the telephone right now!** You may not realize it, but behind the scenes, the parents dealing with illness sometimes literally cry with gratitude and relief at this oh-so-simple gesture.

- **Best friends are especially helpful, and now isn't the wisest time to challenge our children's choices.** (Of course, if those best friends are engaged in illicit behavior or if you feel concern when your child is supervised by the friend's parents, this advice to be tolerant should be thrown in the garbage.) **It helps kids so much to have a trusted and loving peer in whom to confide.** When a best friend relationship already exists, the respective adults are wise to make an extra effort to keep it strong and steady—to be extra flexible about chauffeur service and sleepovers (yes, even on school nights). We help tremendously when we allow these friends to be together, to talk together, to study and do chores and play together, for hours at a time, uninterrupted. **Obviously, it helps most when the family who *isn't* living directly with the illness offers to bear the brunt of the driving and adult supervision.**

- **Families like mine also need and appreciate the healthy adults in our lives who befriend our children.** We honestly feel like basket cases much of the time, struggling with such powerful emotions and the incredible new adjustments we are forced to make. It is such a relief when our children have other responsible adults to turn to—people who aren't edgy and impatient and losing their tempers over the silly little things that would have made us chuckle before this illness struck the family.

- **If you are an adult outside the incurably ill family** who has already developed a special bond with such a child, take the time to deepen it. Or, if a relationship like this has the chance of developing, nurture it.

When I think back to what we went through when my husband was so sick, one woman comes to mind—Peggy Jergens. She was the mother of my daughter's best friend, Katie. The girls had been inseparable since sixth grade, and there were a few months in there where my daughter Linda lived at the Jergenses' house more often than she did with us. Weekends, school nights. . . . She stopped home every day, but she basically lived over there, for days at a time. At first I felt guilty because the Jergenses had six kids and not much money, and I worried about Linda being a drain and yet another mouth to feed. But Peggy never let me give her a thing—we never even really talked about the arrangement in a formal way. And she never tried to act like she was Linda's mother; I never once felt jealous or like I was being replaced. Peggy just made sure the girls did their chores, she made sure Linda did her schoolwork, she drove the girls to all their activities. And those last few months when I was up three and four times a night, I would cry and feel sorry, and then I would think of my sweet Linda, snug and sleeping, well-fed, homework done, in a house full of happy, rowdy kids. And I would feel better. So much more than grateful. I thank God for Peggy Jergens. I never even knew her very well, but I don't know how we could have done it without her.

- **Perhaps the most difficult situation occurs when the incurable person in the family is a child.** Some special considerations for this most treacherous of journeys:

- **Be honest with the child.** When s/he asks, "Am I going to die?" find a way to tell the truth. Most children older than three already realize what's happening. *Please,* give them the chance to talk about their journey with the people they trust and love most deeply. Otherwise they travel alone—which is terrifying for most *adults* to do.

- **During periods of hospitalization, be sure to have time as an entire family, and *daily.*** For example, if parents need to stay at the hospital, find a friend who can drive the rest of the family over every evening so they can have dinner together.

- **Parents are very clumsy at comforting each other.** We could think of them as two mountain climbers. A rock slide crashes down on them; they survive but each is badly broken. There they lay on their respective rocky ledges, each in unbearable pain but unable to help the other. They need *others* to help them, and even then there is no guarantee for a safe and easy descent.

- **Mothers and fathers feel this pain differently.** Moms and dads relate to their children in very special ways. And each parent is perhaps envious of that unique relationship enjoyed by the *other* parent. There is often jealousy that the mother has had more physical contact with the child, or that the father has had more play time with the child.

- **A relationship between spouses can be ripped apart when their child is ill or dies.** This is especially true when circumstances cause one parent to blame the other, the mother who carries hemophilia to her son, for example.

- **Siblings need special attention when a child is ill, but they often don't get it.** Their parents are in too much pain *themselves* to be of much help. And other relatives tend to focus their major efforts toward supporting the parents. Helpful friends and loved ones make a special effort to reach out to the sisters and brothers of an incurable child.

- **Grandparents are often the true forgotten grievers.** When a child is ill, the parents often make medical decisions without consulting the grandparents, even though the grandparents may have tremendous knowledge and hold valuable opinions about these matters.

- **We sometimes fail to acknowledge the depth of a grandparent's loss, but in fact grandparents hurt on two levels;** they stand to lose their own relationship with their grandchild. They also hurt for *their* child, who is now in unspeakable pain. How hard it is, for any parent to stand by and watch while their children—and their children's children—make this journey.

- **One of the most thoughtless things we can say to a parent** is "God needs another rose for his garden." Worse is the comment, "At least you have other children."

- **Many close-to-death children say they are physically tired of the struggle and ready to "let go," but they can't because they know how their families will hurt.** At times the most loving thing a family can do is to directly tell the child, "It's okay—you can go. We'll always love you and keep you with us in our hearts but we want you to do what must be done."

- **When a child is lost, we have to wait for healing,** sometimes for a lifetime. We need patience. By the same token, **many families are strengthened by this experience**—the power of their coping mechanisms amazes them, their love and loyalty are deepened, and their spirits are awakened through sharing and eventually surmounting this incredible pain.

- To end this chapter on a self-indulgent note, I'm aware it's far too long; I've struggled to make it shorter. I've finally realized the verbosity is because of our nine-year-old daughter. Her very existence makes this illness experience even harder. *And* her very existence inspires my husband and me to do the best job possible with the lives we've been given. **Godspeed to the children of families facing incurable illness.**

NOTES

10

SPIRIT AND RITUAL—
SIGNPOSTS ON OUR JOURNEY

- **In almost every culture, serious illness is viewed as an event that has some spiritual significance.** And in nearly every culture, many people feel their loved ones have some sort of presence or in some special way continue on, after life. **But the ways in which we spiritually *interpret* these experiences varies tremendously.** In fact, our beliefs are sometimes so contradictory we fight wars over them.

- **Helpful friends and loved ones allow the incurably ill family to follow their own life choices, philosophies, and behaviors.** For example, the ill husband who avoids his parish might tell his wife that mass just doesn't awaken him; he feels more spiritually alive when he has a few hours of solitude and time for private reverie.

- **How we define ourselves philosophically and spiritually is deeply personal. In every way, we must take extra care not to impose our *own* views onto other people.** When talking to patients and their loved ones, we need to avoid offering our own definitions of illness, dying, the "hereafter," etc. It's better to just listen, even when we consider what we're hearing to be "heresy." Input about our own spiritual beliefs isn't especially necessary or comforting.

There is one condolence letter I will never forget. The person wrote, "Your father is so much happier now that he's in heaven. He's with his Maker, where he always wanted to be."

That letter disgusted me. My father was agnostic, maybe even an atheist. I don't think he even believed in heaven. And I know for certain he wouldn't be happiest there. He'd much rather be with his buddies in the club house, drinking a beer after 18 holes of golf.

She should have left her "God" out of my condolence letter.

- **Instead, encourage the other person to define their spiritual experience—with no judgment or argument.** We help most when we let them use us as a sounding board, to verbalize and clarify their thoughts and feelings. Instead of telling, *ask.* Use gentle probing questions. Gently nod and smile to encourage them to continue. Take special care not to monopolize the airtime. (See Listening and Responding with All Our Senses, p. 91.)

- **Humor can be dangerous, especially when we're less than familiar with a person's culture, philosophy, or spirituality.** Our jokes are easily misinterpreted; sometimes they backfire. "I guess your parents agreed with the pope on birth control" might seem like a harmlessly lighthearted remark to make toward a Catholic friend with many siblings. But deep inside, that friend could be very offended. It's wiser to allow time to pass and lots of trust to develop before truly exercising our funnybones.

- **When we reach out to a family of a different religion, ethnicity, or culture**, it helps to find out as much as we can about their approaches to illness, dying, and grief.

A good friend from my college circle died in a car accident when she was only thirty-three. She'd been raised Jewish, but none of us had ever really talked much about religion. So I was grateful when another close friend in the circle, also raised Jewish, called to tell me not to send flowers. I wouldn't have known, otherwise.

- **It also helps to consider: Are there areas or issues where you might feel moral or ethical conflict?** For instance, your sister is "living in sin" with her lover, who is now seriously ill and (you feel) draining her financially as well as physically. Or a cousin calls a family meeting, tells his loved ones he is gay, and that his partner—who everybody used to think was "just a friend"—is HIV positive. Are there any ways in which you feel judgmental, even subtly?

Once I asked a gay friend, living with AIDS, if there were any irritations he felt being treated by a heterosexual medical team. I wanted to know if there were ways his doctors and nurses might be unintentionally hurtful. He said, "I've gotten really good care. I've always felt respected; in fact, some of my team even came to Jeff's and my anniversary party, although they may have thought it was strange. But there is one thing that bugs me: they'll call him my friend. 'I'd like you to meet Michael and his friend, Jeff.' Or, 'Will your friend, Jeff, be coming to the appointment with you?' It makes me want to scream, because we've been together for twenty-five years and he's my spouse, my soulmate, my lover, my partner. I couldn't be doing this without him. He is so much more than just my friend."

• **When we find ourselves feeling critical, we need to be especially cautious about getting into philosophical or spiritual discussions.** We avert many problems by remembering that *accepting someone is not the same as agreeing* with them. We can choose to let our differences slide. The incurable family needs stability right now—not friends who try to shake the foundations of their very values.

• **To open ourselves to other cultures, philosophies, and definitions of spirituality, it is best to begin by thinking about our own beliefs,** to examine our own foundations, rather than taking them for granted. What makes us who we are? What values, attitudes, behaviors, and stereotypes do we bring to any interaction? What are our spiritual biases? How does our cultural and spiritual heritage affect our daily lives—what rituals are important to us?

- **As we look to our lives, we'll note that we exercise our spirits in many ways—some formal and ceremonial, some spontaneous.** One family attends church services every Sunday. Another takes a fun-loving walk on a nature trail. A third spends the first Saturday of every month cleaning dorms at the local homeless shelter. Any time we pause to consider our connections, the gifts of the universe, or our contributions to our community, we are being spiritual.

- **Perhaps an atheist would prefer a word without religious connotations, but in my view, the word *spirit* has little to do with formal religion. Spirituality is something experienced by everybody.** It's that profound combination of energy and appreciation and incredulity, enveloped by a desire to make our world a better place. Walk outside during any moonlit night. Visit the children's ward in a hospital. Sing with your sister. These can be spiritual experiences.

- **A healthy perspective is one that seeks out the soul in everyday events**—to find deeper meaning in the mundane, to notice the world on a moment-by-moment basis. For instance, as we load the dryer we imagine those who invented it, we consider their excitement as the idea developed, and we smile with appreciation. Later, we notice a beautiful shaft of sunlight darting on the nearby wall. Our task takes on a new dimension—*soul*. (See Moore, *Care of the Soul*.)

- **Spirit and soul is everywhere around us. We often find it in our daily rituals, those life habits that ground and define us.** Rituals are those certain things we do in an orderly and meaningful fashion. For instance, one man starts each day by reading the funnies first, then he turns to the editorials. Next door, a mother sings the same soothing lullaby to her children, every single night. A third neighbor goes grocery shopping every Saturday morning, but before setting out, she first stops at her parents' house for a visit and a cup of coffee. Such rituals bring soul and spirit to daily events—without them, morning or bedtime or grocery shopping just isn't the same.

- **Such rituals become interrupted and sometimes even obliterated when a family lives with incurable illness.** It's impossible to sing to our other kids when we're virtually living at the hospital watching over the second born. And we can't take time to stop for coffee with our parents on Saturdays now, when a bedridden husband waits at home. In fact most Saturdays, we can scarcely manage the grocery shopping at all.

- **When old rituals and routines are tossed overboard during this journey, it helps to recall that we can create *new* rituals at any time.** Our parents now come to *our* house for coffee on Saturdays—and in truly helpful households, they arrive after doing our grocery shopping, too. Or the man still drinks coffee and reads his paper in the morning, but his ill wife likes the funnies first; these days, he starts with the sports section, and later, they'll tackle the crossword puzzle—together. **Good friends and loved ones encourage us to be *flexible* rather than *frustrated* when illness forces us to alter the routines and rituals that have always been so important to us.**

- **In virtually every society, special types of ritual exist—those for *purely ceremonial* purposes.** The infant's head is anointed with holy water, the educated person walks across the platform to shake hands and accept a rolled-up diploma, the man and woman pledge their love before a congregation. Such rituals are designed to help participants mark the meanings and emotions of an important experience; they are often conducted (but not always) in the company of a supportive community. **These types of ceremonies can be created and changed, too,** and doing so can add powerful soul-force to a family experiencing illness. It can help when they officially mark the more significant episodes and issues of this journey, such as hair loss, remission, final treatments, etc.

- **When creating a ritual, think specifically about what you want to say or accomplish.** Perhaps we want to appreciate our ill mother for all she's done for others—and *now,* while she can hear our thanks—so we spend the morning of her birthday cleaning out her garage, giving the bounty to the Salvation Army. Or, perhaps we would like to get rid of ancient hurts and angers toward a seriously ill loved one, so we write them all down on a piece of paper, privately read each out loud, hold the paper over the sink, and burn it.

- **Find a symbolic connection between the activity you choose and the specific idea you wish to express.**

  - *Plant a tree or shrub to symbolize growth, nurturing, effort, and reward with faith that the patient will see it bloom*

  - *Light candles, a fire in the fireplace, a huge community bonfire, to symbolize warmth, the light of truth and knowledge*

  - *Shoot off fireworks to draw attention—use them also to ward off evil spirits (which was in fact their original use, back in medieval China)*

  - *Fast for twenty-four hours to symbolize sacrifice, suffering, cleansing from past wrongs and injuries*

  - *Feast at an all-night party to symbolize reward, triumph, new beginnings, such as the patient getting word of remission*

  - *Shred and burn old clothing or documents, smash or destroy belongings that mark a painful time, as symbols of moving forward or saying farewell to the past*

  - *Exchange gifts, songs, tributes, poems, awards, to symbolize a patient's life's passages, endeavors, loves, and loyalties*

  - *Wear special clothing, eat special foods, to commemorate important events or their anniversaries, such as a final treatment*

  - *Gather the family and clean up a park, or sing at a nursing home, to symbolize gratitude to the community*

- **When creating and then suggesting a ritual to others, we need to carefully consider the audience.** Group participation can certainly make a ceremonial gesture more powerful; it can also cause the event to backfire when the players approach the event with insincerity or ridicule. If they imply that it is too hokey or if we feel foolish or uncomfortable in their presence, they shouldn't be there.

- **Certainly some patients and family members balk at the idea of these rituals.** They say, "Well, maybe I'd plant a tree. But the rest of this hogwash is just pure, primitive symbolism—nothing but a total waste of time. Why not do something *worthwhile,* instead!?" Such family members can **exercise their spirituality in other ways**, like giving speeches to school kids once a month, or making the private commitment to make someone else laugh, every single day. Such activities can become our life's rituals, too.

- **Rituals needn't be serious and heavy.** Have *fun* when designing them. For instance, acknowledge your daughter's difficult treatments by buying her a tiny teddy bear for each time she has to take radiation. When she's finally completed her protocol, she'll have a basketful of loving friends to remind her just how far she's come. Or, celebrate your brother's remission by having a huge kite-flying party.

- And of course, **many rituals are better left completely private**—ripping old photographs or letters, for instance, or priming ourselves to visit a hospitalized child by playing her favorite kiddy tape in the car and singing along at the top of our lungs.

- **Sometimes we'll create a ritual, perform it, then find it doesn't satisfy.** We feel "ho hum" or even silly and may be tempted to dismiss the whole idea as wacky. Instead, come up with another idea and *try again.* Some rituals are like going to a restaurant and choosing a dessert that looked and sounded scrumptious, but tasting it was a total disappointment. That doesn't mean we'll avoid dessert altogether the next time. We'll just choose something different.

- **Rituals are our signposts; they mark our family path.** And every family celebrates soul and spirit in unique ways. This one eats birthday cakes for breakfast. That one has pickup pizza every Friday night. When these signposts return, they remind us to take stock. For example, how is our family doing today, compared to the family we were on Pizza Night last week?

- **Serious illness alters some of our most treasured rituals and traditions, it's true,** but why not put a candle in Jell-O for one family member and serve breakfast birthday cake to the others? And why not pick up the pizza and gather at the hospital to enjoy it? We can revere our traditions, short of putting them on a pedestal. They'll survive being shaken up a bit. Sometimes that's even *good* for them.

We had Thanksgiving at my grandmother's house as usual this year, but this time she didn't spend four days making it. Instead, we all brought the food, and we actually ate it on TV trays around her bed. It's a family tradition that everyone makes speeches of gratitude after dinner, even the little ones, and it's also sort of a family joke that my father's speech is always way too sappy and long-winded. After the last speech, we clap for everyone, and then we have dessert.

Grandma was dozing on and off through the meal and the speeches, but she woke up when she heard the clapping. She looked sort of startled at first, like, "Where am I?" Then she got her bearings and said, "Oh no, did I fall asleep and miss Roger's entire speech?" She got this devilish little twinkle in her eye and said, "Well, I guess even I have something to be thankful for this year!" We were all surprised at first, then my father started to laugh and clap, and the rest of us joined in. And six months later, we still crack up about Grandma's Thanksgiving Speech.

I know we probably won't be able to have Thanksgiving at Grandma's house at all next year. But I have a feeling we'll be laughing about her speech for many more Thanksgivings to come.

11

EUPHEMISM, METAPHOR, AND THE WORDS OF ILLNESS

- **The words we choose have a huge effect on those around us. Even one little verb or noun can completely alter a person's attitudes about her situation.** For instance, once I took a hospice patient to her doctor's appointment; she had been feeling new pressures in her torso. On the ride home she told me, "First he felt my abdomen, then my chest, and then he said, "Yes, you're right. It's *growing*." She cried all the way home. She kept saying, "It's growing. It's *growing*." She was depressed for days. I thought to myself, how much easier this would have been if that well-meaning doctor had left out just one awful word and instead commented, "You're right, I feel it here, too."

- **Some words carry a heavy emotional punch. We could think of them as "loaded."** But things get confusing because words that are loaded to one person are harmless to another. After all, many patients might hear the word *growing* and not be fazed in the least. Or, think of the scores of people you know who use the expression, "Oh, God!" Now, think of the others you know who consider it blasphemy. **Helpful friends and loved ones play it safe. We take care to choose words that are as value-*neutral* as possible.**

I'm on a personal mission to wipe out the word "terminal" when people talk about incurable illness. I've worked in hospice ten years and nearly everyone I know uses the term. I guess I'll be fighting an uphill battle. But the word has always bothered me—it's so negative. And it pulls everyone's focus toward death, not life. After all, what does terminal mean? The end.

When my daughter got sick, that word truly began to trouble me, so I felt compelled to start my mission. When people say, "She's terminal," I try to make them understand. She's incurable, not terminal. After all, we're all "terminal."

- **We help by adapting our language to mirror that of the individual patient's and family members'.** We listen for the other person's style, vocabulary, even his use of metaphors. For instance, we notice if people use slang, we notice if they use flowery language or more concrete terms. We wait to see if they are humorous or sentimental. Are they exceptionally polite and formal? Are they casual? In short, we **listen for *their* language preferences, and allow *their* style to set the tone of all conversation.**

- ***Euphemism* is a specific example of such adapting.** When the family speaks in euphemisms, they choose softer or less direct language to express difficult or painful issues. For instance, some people say "She passed on yesterday" rather than "She died yesterday." We help by listening for euphemisms, and *using them ourselves* if the patient or loved one seems to prefer them.

I remember my early days of hospice nursing, when we used to sit around self-righteously saying, "When someone dies, we should say so. We need to use the word 'death' as professionals as often as we can, so the world will catch up with us and become more accepting."

But now I have more life experience than I care to admit. And we were wrong back then. For instance, there's the patient I cared for just last month. She had cancer for eight years before she came into hospice, and she was one of the most accepting people I've known. She was very comfortable talking about her death; we talked about it more frankly than I do with most patients. But I never once heard her use the word "cancer" and she never once said anything direct about dying. She called it "my problem" and she talked about "not being around." That's as close to saying it as she got.

It would have been stupid of me to go shouting the words "cancer" and "death" in every conversation. Normally I do use those words, but with this patient, I just called it her "problem," too.

- **There are issues other than language. Helpful loved ones refuse to become irritated when they have to repeat or clarify the same thing several times.** Families in this situation have difficulty hearing things because they are already on info overload, dealing with so much that is new and uncertain. For instance, you asked your nephew to pick up some laxatives for his father, he even said yes, but he later comes home empty-handed, denying that he ever heard your request. Avoid argument or frustration; just return to the pharmacy.

- **It is also normal—though frustrating—when family members confuse or distort something they've heard, then repeat it to someone else.** "Aunt Alice told me all of Dad's pain medications are sold over the counter," your niece relays to her brother. What you *really* said was, "The pills I want you to pick up are sold over the counter." We mustn't become frustrated when we have to clarify things we thought others already understood.

- **It also helps to find new ways to say the same old thing**—for the sake of interest as well as reinforcement. "Time for your magic potion," "How about a little nectar?" and the ever-popular "Down the hatch" are all livelier ways of saying, "Take your medicine."

- **Supportive people know the difference between *repetition* and *paraphrase,* and we use whichever technique helps most in the current situation.** We ask ourselves, does the family need me to *clarify* existing information? Or do they need me to *obtain more* in-depth information?

  REPETITION: when we "play back" to the speaker something that was already said, *almost verbatim.* Repetition is helpful when we need to clarify tangible facts and dates, to reinforce instructions, etc.

> EXAMPLE: *"So, the nurse says to double my mealtime dose and that might provide a full night's sleep?"* asks the patient.
> *"That's exactly right. Double your current dose at mealtime,"* repeats her caretaker husband. (He verifies and reinforces.)

PARAPHRASE: when we "play back" to the speaker something that was already said, *intentionally changing the words originally chosen,* because we want to obtain more information about the underlying ideas, thoughts, values, attitudes, concerns, philosophies, spiritual considerations, etc.

> EXAMPLE: *"I was so angry when the nurse didn't call back,"* a caretaker says.
> *"You were frustrated because she didn't seem concerned?"* the friend paraphrases.
> *"No, I was irritated with the clinic, because once again, I don't think they gave her my message,"* explains the caretaker. (Through paraphrase, the friend encourages the caretaker to further clarify her first, somewhat ambiguous statement.)

- **One of our most useful language devices is metaphor.** For instance, we speak of the *battle* with cancer, being *invaded* by bad cells, *nuking* the cancer cells. These symbolic descriptions conjure up powerful images that help us define our experiences.

- **Metaphors are extremely powerful—they make excellent vehicles for emphasizing and clarifying ideas.** For example, hospice research has found patients are more likely to take their pain medications correctly when the nurse creates an "educational" metaphor instead of just "medically prescribing." Consider the following:

Imagine a hilltop in California, an area prone to drought and fires. If that area gets rain—even a tiny bit every few days—a fire could start but it probably won't last. It would be easy to put out. But now think of that same hillside after months of drought.

No rain at all. When the fire starts, it begins to blaze immediately. It covers the hilltop in record time, and there's virtually nothing anyone can do except stand back and watch.

Pain is like that fire. And medications are like the rain. Patients must take their gentle pain medications on a regular basis, whether or not they actually feel pain. Just like the hilltop needs a tiny bit of rain, even when things are already damp and green. That way, if a major fire does erupt, we can quickly get the pain under control.

- **Patients often use extremely symbolic talk, especially in the final months of illness.** It's that talk that sometimes seems "crazy" or confused to caregivers, but generally it holds the key to powerful information. **Listen to the patient's metaphors.** Does the ill person talk about visiting someone? Coming home? Walking up stairs? Do they look for objects in their imagination—a lost cow, a long-deceased pet or cousin, an old ring or photograph? What real-life concerns might be symbolized? **Step into these metaphors, even the ones that seem to border on dementia.** For instance, instead of saying, "Ma, there's no cow here—we're in your bedroom," try asking, "What color is the cow? What is its name? When did you see it last?" Find out about the cow, and we just might find out about a real-life concern or longing. (See Callanan and Kelley, *Final Gifts*.)

- **Helpful friends listen for the caregivers' metaphors, too.** How family members choose to symbolically describe their situation can give us lots of insights into their morale, perspectives, and coping mechanisms. For example, one family member says she's drowning. Another says he's chugging along. A third says she's riding a roller-coaster. Each description carries implications and insights.

I remember one family from our support group who was very musical—every one of them played an instrument. They were talking one night about their horrible arguments, and another group member said, "You folks are just like an orchestra. Sometimes one of you gets a little out of tune, that's all." The idea seemed to stick somehow. Every week they'd walk in the room and someone would say, "Oh, good, the orchestra has arrived!" Pretty soon they started to talk that way themselves. Instead of sounding so angry, the wife started saying, "Bob is sure playing from a different score sheet!" Everyone laughed and the whole idea seemed like a joke, but deep down it really bonded them, too. And they found a way of talking about their problems that didn't attack each other.

- **We needn't necessarily share the metaphors we invent.** Metaphors can be equally useful when we keep them to ourselves, a private tool for making sense and meaning of this demanding—and phenomenal—journey.

- **The final pages of this chapter provide some symbolic ways to think about living with incurable illness.** Perhaps some of these metaphors will ring true for a family you know and love.

The River

The family finds itself suddenly adrift in the river of incurable illness. Loved ones and friends watch from the riverbanks. The medical team reels in the family, giving guidance and provisions when they're able. There are stagnant times, times of spinning in eddies. There are gently gliding times, enjoying the scenery, and terrifying times of relapse and rapids. Beneath it all is the knowledge that we could capsize; we have little control over the current. This experience is a journey, sometimes frightening, sometimes peaceful, sometimes exhilarating. This metaphor can inspire the family to take up an oar. It can also help them sit back to appreciate an experience even when they can't entirely control it.

Foundations

The family is a building, an edifice. How well is it built? What values, attitudes, beliefs, and traditions are supporting them? Is the fortress of this family built on sand? stone? mud? And what is in the environment of this family structure? Are they isolated—a crumbling castle made of stone, isolated on a Yorkshire mountaintop? Or is the family edifice just one part of a larger, close-knit community, like Mesa Verde? What is this family's infrastructure? How strong is the mortar of their relationships, emotions, history, functionality, conflicts. How well do they maintain their property? Do they attend to the tiny cracks and creeping weeds before they become insurmountable problems? Or is the family fortress disintegrating with neglect? If the shelter or protection of the family is weak in any way, the family can talk about ways to strengthen it—adding support beams, patching the roof, building an addition, deciding to move, etc.

The Circus

The illness appears in the community as a complete surprise, just as the circus one day rolls into a sleepy rural town. The family members become the performers. They are brave and proud, taking risks, walking wires. They find they must trust others completely—family members, the medical team—just as the trapeze artist has to operate on the faith that his partner will catch him. Though fearful, these performers say to themselves, "If I have to do this, let me do it well." Their community is the crowd of onlookers, scared and thrilled, marveling at the control and feats and heroics of these performers. The circus metaphor is especially meaningful to families where posturing is important, those families who operate best by hiding the clown's tears, and who approach their community with a behind-the-scenes credo: "It's showtime, performers! And the show *must* go on!"

The Wild

We all have a certain instinctual and primitive nature, just as animals in the jungle. We are territorial and competitive; some species take more extreme positions on their boundaries than others. We are capable of camouflaging our true colors—sometimes to hide from something bigger, sometimes to prey on others. We give birth and protect our young with ferocity, but some families throw progeny from the nest sooner than others; some even destroy their weaker members. We engage in an amazing array of nonverbal behaviors—touch, vocal cues, power stances, eye contact. Some of us retreat during conflict, others take the offensive. This metaphor can be enlightening to patients with complicated personal relationships. It can clarify our notions of "the enemy," and it also brings new perspective to survival of the fittest philosophies.

The Weather

Every life is lived through seasons—from the spring of childhood to the winter of accumulated age. For some families, winter comes far too early. Serious illness is much like the changing weather. The seasonal changes of illness are recurring—cycles of relapse and remission, the chemo every fourteen days. We move through different phases in our illness, just as summer follows spring. We learn to take comfort in these returning seasons, even though we always have to adjust for them. On the other hand, the storms of change can be terrifying and permanent, like the hurricane that razes the town or the surgery that removes a patient's arm. This metaphor can help families consider the "atmosphere" that surrounds them. How pure is the air? Is there sufficient warmth, water? Where can they seek shelter in the storm? How can they best prepare for a hard winter?

Bridges

We spend our lives building and crossing bridges, creating connections between ourselves and other people. Some of our interpersonal bridges are major—like the New York Triboro—a convoluted central artery of primary relationships. Other bridges in our lives are minor; we can choose not to cross because we have other options. Like an acquaintance who isn't that essential to us, a casual conversation with a co-worker, we aren't too concerned when these bridges burn. Bridges, just like personalities and conversations, are sometimes meandering; the Golden Gate and the Tappan Zee curl you around and show off the scenery. Other conversational styles are straight to the point, just like the George Washington Bridge, which takes a beeline to its destination. Before deciding whether to cross, it helps to consider the engineering. Is it sturdy? Will it hold up? After all, some bridges, just like some relationships, aren't worth it. They only lead us to the wrong destination. Some bridges are complicated; the interpersonal signs are hard to read, the entrances and exits and overpasses become confusing. Other bridges are terrifying; the frayed rope path that stretches over the mountain ravine, like the conversation in which you have to tell a child she might not live long. This conversational bridge shakes and sways and feels anything but safe, but sometimes we have no other choice but to cross. The bridges metaphor reminds families to meet each other halfway, and to coax others across through initiation techniques. This metaphor also helps families make sense of serious conflicts and irreconcilable relationships—while it hurts to stand by and watch as loved ones sever ties, it isn't our job to ensure that others "patch things up." We can act as stepping stones between two feuding loved ones, but we can't force them to cross.

Quilting

Few metaphors are more American than that of the quilting bee, where friends and neighbors gather to stitch and socialize, threading their lives together while they work. Such is the circle of loved ones, surrounding a family with incurable illness. Friends arrive on the doorstep with only scraps for resources, but through collaboration, they produce function and, frequently, unusual artistry. Some quilts are carefully planned and measured, just like some illnesses. Others are called Crazy Quilts, the shapes spilling out on top of each other, just like some illnesses that randomly toss down their symptoms and consequences. Some quilters are more experienced—those friends who help the family with tactful efficiency. Other quilters make uneven or insecure stitches—the friends who stumble through an awkward conversation, but their parts of the finished product are no less precious. The idea of quilting can help families accept assistance from others. It honors teamwork, and it appreciates the individual "signatures" of every quilter who helps out.

NOTES

12

LISTENING AND RESPONDING
WITH ALL OUR SENSES

- **It's been said before, and for good reason: Listening is the single most important thing we can do for each other.** We must listen well to each family member, we must listen to each loved one, we must listen to medical professionals providing guidance, and more. **It helps to listen with *all our senses.*** Humans can gather powerful information in every interaction, especially when they pay attention to sight, smell, touch, taste, in addition to sound. And as necessary as these five senses are, we are even better listeners when we **develop a sixth — intuition.**

- **Labels we give to other people (bureaucrat, yuppie doctor, hypochondriac) get in the way of our listening. And few labels are more emotionally charged than this one: dying person.** The world whispers this label, sometimes from the moment a person is diagnosed with an incurable illness. The label is powerful; it alters or even eliminates many of the family's former friendships. Helpful friends remember that everyone is a dying person.

- **Listening and response go hand in hand.** After all, we don't get much mileage from monologues. We *react* and *respond* to what others say, both with our words and our body language. **Helpful friends and loved ones pay careful attention to the feedback we provide.**

- **The feedback is more than merely a response; it actually *changes* the messages to follow.** If our reactions judge or evaluate what was said, the patient or loved one will feel compelled to change the conversation or perhaps even stop talking before she really wanted to. But if our feedback is free of evaluation or judgment, we encourage the loved one to communicate more freely and fully. Imagine this conversation with your friend who is caring for her ill husband.

SHE: "I'm just so tired, I think I'll explode."

YOU: "That's such a normal feeling, and nothing to feel guilty about, Marge. Perhaps your sister could come to help you."

or

YOU: "I see. Tell me more about it."

Both replies are good ones, but only the second response allows the caregiver to explore and solve her own problems (and gives her more control). **Sometimes friends mistakenly try to help by solving problems too quickly, before family members have had a chance to discuss and resolve the problems for themselves.**

- **Listening occurs at five different levels, each requiring greater energy and involvement.** It's like walking up steps: The higher you climb, the greater your need for stamina.

- **Close friends are often required to listen to the patient or family at the very top step, using active empathy and sometimes even counseling skills.** This is hard work! What makes it most difficult is that, when listening at this level, we *have to hold in our opinions.*

- **It is important to note that top-step listening requires more energy and much more time.** In the previous example, it would be hard to invite a friend to "tell me more" if our friend mentioned "exploding" at the *end* of our time together, while our son was waiting to be driven to soccer practice. **We mustn't feel guilty when we make the decision to refrain from top-level listening but it does help to explain:** "Marge, these feelings sound important, but Mike needs to get to practice, and I can't give it my full attention right now." **When we postpone an important conversation, we help most when we remember to set a *specific* time in the future:** "Can we talk about this later, Marge?" is not

LISTENING LEVELS: THE STEPS MODEL

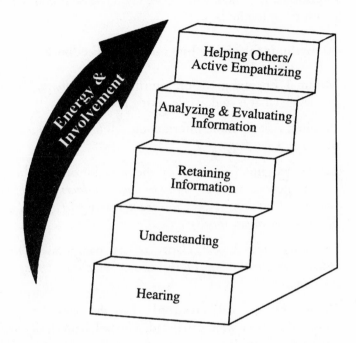

as effective as "Could I come over for coffee at ten-thirty tomorrow, so we can talk about this then?"

- **Providing a judgment-free atmosphere obviously means holding back our negative opinions** ("That doesn't sound like it will work!"). **Surprisingly, it also means holding back our favorable reactions** ("What a *great* idea!"). When we give a "Go for it!" to someone too early, it keeps him too focused on that one "good" idea and hinders him in exploring other options, thoughts, and feelings.

- **It's also wise to avoid changing the subject,** even when the conversation is awkward, stilted, halting, or otherwise uncomfortable. The most supportive friend allows the patient or family member to decide when it's time to move on to other topics.

- **The quickest way to stop a conversation is to provide advice and opinions.** But then, what *do* we say? Helpful friends develop skill with these methods:

- **Seven methods for giving Judgment-Free Feedback:**

    Minimal Encourager: Soft murmurs, *"Um-hmm,"* to acknowledge what is said, while taking little airtime.

    Probing: Ask for more information. *"What did you say next?"* or *"Then what happened?"*

    Acknowledging: Comment on the behavior of the other person in a neutral manner. *"I can see your shoulders get tight when you talk about this."* (Note: You are *not* saying, *"I agree. I would be tense, too, about this."*)

    Checking Out: Repeat, clarify, reflect, paraphrase. *"You say this is the fourth time in the past week they've changed her prescription?"*

    Paraphrase: Use *different* words than the ones the speaker chose, and restate what you heard. This will help clarify underlying values, hidden attitudes, or unverbalized assumptions. *"So, there were feelings of anger, or maybe sadness, because he didn't answer your letter?"*

    Repetition: Use the same words the speaker chose, and repeat verbatim what you heard. This will help clarify specific terms, tangible "contract" issues, and verify the accuracy of statements. *"So, her specific words were, 'in three to four weeks,' is that right?"*

    Summarizing: A combination of all the techniques except probing, in which you pull together the main ideas you heard in a concise paragraph or two. This is a very useful closure tool; it marks the end of judgment-free feedback time and helps the person move into evaluating the situation. After a summary statement, help the person generate solutions and make decisions.

- **The first two methods (minimal encourager, probing) are the easiest and also the *safest*.** All they require is that friends *keep quiet as much as possible;* and when they *do* talk, they turn the conversation *back* to the patient or loved one.

It really is true that lots of people ask how you are but they don't want to hear my side of it—they just want to tell me theirs. Anyway, you start to tell them things and their eyes glaze over. They start telling me about someone else they know. Or something that happened to them. Or worse, they start giving me advice. So when people ask me how I am, I usually say, "Fine, things are the same," and change the subject.

Luckily I have one friend who lets me say whatever is on my mind. She doesn't get uncomfortable when I start to cry, she doesn't try to "fix" me. She isn't always struggling to say the right thing. In fact, I guess she sometimes hardly talks at all.

If you think about it, what she does isn't so tough. Instead of trying so hard to find something to say, she just sits and listens. I wish more people were like her.

- **Helpful friends monitor the airtime. Hopefully, *we* aren't using too much of it.** We share comments and anecdotes only because they are pertinent, and whenever we wish to share a story we first ask ourselves, "Am I saying this for *his* sake, or for *mine*?" As good friends, we are careful not to be self-indulgent in the stories we tell.

- **Our feedback sometimes "judges" others, even when we're trying hard *not* to.** Usually this happens through our tone of voice rather than the words we use. For instance, practice all the ways we could say a simple "um-hmm"—a supposedly *easy* minimal encourager:

"Um-HMMM . . ." (surprise)
"Um-hmmmm . . ." (skepticism)
"UM-hmmm . . ." (agreement)
"Um-hm . . ." (sarcasm)

- **It also helps to know that a person hearing our judgment-free feedback feels very comfortable and *often believes we agree* with what they're saying. This can be dangerous later!** "But you *said* you thought my mother was being shortsighted about going into hospice . . . well, you certainly never *disagreed* with me!!?" At these confusing moments, an important communication principle is handy: *Accepting* **ideas isn't the same as** *agreeing* **with them.** Just let the person know, "Your points were well thought and valid. It was helpful to hear them. My own perspective is a bit different, but back then it didn't seem important to argue about it."

- **Being judgment-free isn't best for all conversations with patients and their loved ones. There are lots of times on this journey when we must assess, evaluate, and even correct** the ideas and behaviors of the family. Imagine an aunt who confides she isn't taking her medications. Or a beloved seven-year-old who says she caused her mother's illness. If all we can say to these people is "Um-hmm, tell me more," they might soon be in deep trouble.

- Helpful listeners do assess when there is call for comment, but **first we consciously delay reactions or suggestions.** We begin by giving the family member time to explain, "vent," and share all that they have to say. This enables us to respond to the entire message, rather than just fragments. The more information we have, the better prepared we will be to provide thoughtful assessments or corrections.

- **The word** *you* **evokes ego.** Helpful friends **remove a loved one's ego** *(you)* **from any message that is correcting.** "I was hoping for a return to my phone call" is less attacking than "You didn't return my call." We do **include the ego** *(you)* **when complimenting:** "You have the prettiest smile!" We also **include the** *you* **when**

affirming and encouraging: "You are *not* losing your marbles. In fact, *you're* doing an incredible job with this situation!"

- **When talking with patients and their families, we are wise to avoid the following** words that may appear harmless, but in actuality they evoke defensiveness:

  You/Your   *"You didn't call me back to tell me if I should pick up your father's prescription."*
  Instead try: *"I was concerned because I didn't know if I needed to stop at the pharmacy."*

  Always: *"Your son always forgets to call me back."*
  Instead say: *"Lots of times, I haven't received a call back from Larry."*

  Never: *"She never writes out her instructions so I can read them."*
  Instead: *"It seems like I have a hard time reading these instructions, too much of the time."*

  Why: *"Why do you feel that way?"*
  Instead try: *"I wonder what brings about those feelings?"*

  Should: *"You really should talk to a lawyer about your insurance."*
  Try instead: *"Some people find it helpful to talk to a lawyer about these kinds of insurance concerns."*

- **In general, helpful friends try to avoid giving advice,** refrain from judging reactions or decisions, and let patients and loved ones themselves work through the process of living with this illness. Helpful friends **learn to become comfortable with awkward pauses and long periods of quiet** (this is especially true toward the end of life, when a patient turns inward and rests a lot). Helpful friends **strive to understand, instead of trying to be understood.**

- Helpful friends know that, more often than not, **the most generous gift we can give is our accepting silence.**

NOTES

13

OPENING UP
TO OTHERS

- It is essential for those who care about ill people and their families to become their supportive, trustworthy confidantes. **Helpful friends build trust, make openness a hallmark, and know when to keep a secret.**

- **The basic cornerstone of helping others is acceptance. The most supportive friends** *believe* **what a patient and loved ones say** about family dynamics, coping mechanisms, pain and managing it, spirituality, and more. We do not discount their perceptions or experiences, even mildly. **We also try not to deny the other person's reality,** such as saying to them, "Oh, come on now, you can't really mean that!" Such a response is completely invalidating of the other person's feelings—and a sure way to make her clam up in the future.

- **Both caregivers and patients complain of isolation. Caregivers often feel overworked. True friends reach out to the family in** *tangible* **ways.** We stop by regularly, we do chores and errands without being asked, in short, we try to relieve the family of at least some of their tedious day-to-day responsibilities, while also providing opportunities for family members to simply get away from one another.

- **Helpful people watch out for the trap "What would** *you* **do?"** Hearing this question is our clue to turn the conversation back to *them* as quickly as possible. We say something like, "Well, our situations are a little different. What's going on for *you*?"

- **We need to avoid overdoing descriptions of our own experience;** otherwise, we unintentionally monopolize the airtime. This is especially important for many older generation family members—it's easy to unwittingly dominate the conversation when we have wisdom, experience, and a legacy of family stories to share.

- **Good friends don't chatter for chatter's sake,** especially when the patient or loved one is in a period of true turbulence. It's more helpful to remain quiet. Our silent presence is all that's needed.

When my father was unexpectedly hospitalized, some neighbors offered to drive me from the airport straight to see him—my folks live in the mountains, so it was a two-hour ride to the hospital. The whole time, this woman talked—about nothing. Who they'd had lunch with, her garden, every neighbor. I know she thought she was "keeping my mind off it," but all I really wanted was peace and quiet, and she would not shut up. Those were two of my most painful hours, honestly.

- By the same token, good friends realize **big talk usually starts with small talk.** We avoid feeling frustrated or impatient with the same old boring conversations about the weather, sports, road conditions, etc. Small talk gets us to the big stuff.

- **When initiating difficult topics, the two rules are:**
  1. Ask permission to talk about the topic
  2. Give the person an out at your own expense, rather than his/hers

  For example, say:
  "Can I ask a question, or am I just sticking my nose in again?"
  instead of
  "Is it okay to talk about this, or is it just too painful for you?"
  or
  "I'd like to ask something, but maybe you're not quite ready?"

- **It's generally better to ask *specific* and *direct* initiation questions, rather than inviting the other to talk with an am-**

biguous nicety. For example, asking "How did your son react when he found out about your illness?" is more effective than saying, "If you ever want to talk about anything, just let me know."

A good friend of mine died of brain cancer when she was forty-one. She was a single parent with three teenage kids. A few months before she died, we were having lunch when she suddenly said, "I hate it when people say, 'If you ever want to talk, just call me—anytime. Just let me know.' It's the biggest kiss-off statement I've ever heard. I tell them thanks, but inside I burn a little. I always think to myself, 'Okay, I'll do just that. Tonight, at three o'clock in the morning when I can't sleep because my neck hurts and I'm lying awake petrified that Shannon and Jim and Chris won't be able to sell the house after I'm dead, I'll call you. We'll talk all about it.'"

- **A helpful friend isn't too shy to ask a patient scary questions** such as "Are you afraid?" or "What does it feel like to know you might not live as long as you thought?" Many patients are grateful for the opportunity to verbalize things that they may withhold from the loved ones they want to "protect."

- **Here's a list of excellent questions** for any person experiencing incurable illness. **Ask them:**

  - *"What is this experience like for you?"*

  - *"How is your mother [spouse, child, friend, etc.] reacting to all this?"*

  - *"Do you ever think about what happens 'after'?"*

  - *"Are you having any interesting dreams/ideas/revelations?"*

  - *"How do you prefer to spend this time?"*

  - *"Does this experience have any special meaning for you in a spiritual sense?"*

- *"Do the people you love know what they mean to you and why?"*

- *"Are you ever afraid?"*

- *"What do other people consider to be your greatest accomplishments?"*

- *"What do you consider to be your greatest accomplishments?"*

- *"Are there any regrets? Any 'unfinished' business?"*

- *"How might a person in this situation wish to be spoken of and remembered?"*

- *"What people do you most prefer to see?"*

- *"Is there anyone you haven't seen that you'd like to see?"*

- *"What have been the hardest [easiest, most surprising] parts of all this?"*

- *"What are you learning through all this?"*

- **A person might look at this list with trepidation—"I couldn't ask *that*!" is a first thought.** "I'd be way too embarrassed. It's so presumptuous!" Unfortunately, this is the reaction of nearly every person who is close to the patient and loved ones. That's why it is so essential for those of us who can ask to do so.

- If some of these questions strike us as blunt, it's because they are. Many people might not be comfortable with such a direct approach. But **everyone can ask the first and the last questions.** They are vague and nonthreatening; a patient or family member can take them in any direction. If as friends, we asked only these questions and truly listened to the answers, we could talk for hours.

- **Sometimes, casual friends don't ask personal questions because they decide beforehand, "He wouldn't want to talk to *me* about that; I barely know him!"** Not true. In fact, it is sometimes much easier for a patient or family member to share intimate information with people who *don't* know the history firsthand.

My husband and I talked so much in the beginning. When he was diagnosed, and then when he went through treatment, we covered all the majors—the house, the kids, remarriage, the will, you name it, we covered it. But for the past few years he's been in remission, and we don't talk much at all. I guess we feel all talked out. We don't dwell on his situation. And I'm glad, for the most part. It makes things easier.

But I still think about things. I worry that the cancer will come back. I think about myself, with three kids under the age of twelve. I'm only thirty-three years old. And I have a few regrets. There are things I wish we'd done together, but the kids and our responsibilities came so early. My brain is busy and my heart feels full almost all the time. But who could I talk to about being worried I'll become a widow? Would my husband and friends like to hear me talk about that? I don't think so. Sometimes it's a lot easier to talk to total strangers.

- **We can always back off from a conversation if we feel we've been too forward. We *cannot* back off from a conversation we never have in the first place.** And even the shiest people usually enjoy talking about themselves one on one, so long as they don't feel laughed at, judged, or analyzed.

- A good, nonthreatening way to help people start talking is to **ask about prized possessions, collections, hobbies,** etc. When we visit, we look at the surroundings and talk about what we see. **Asking to look at photo albums is another good technique;** it can lead to a visit rich with stories, as the patient and loved ones review and celebrate a lifetime of experience and memories. **If asking to look at photos of family members feels too forward, a friend or acquaintance can try asking to look at pictures of objects the person has mentioned.** "Do you have any pictures of that cabin your family built?" "Did you ever take any pictures of your garden?" These photos will likely lead to others.

- **Sharing stories is a wonderful tool for gaining trust.** Telling a quick story about ourselves will help open the door, but remember that the main objective is to hear about *them.* Our stories can be used as a method for evoking *theirs.* **Ask for stories.** "Tell me how you and Susan met." "How did you get started in your career?" "What was it like to be in the army during the war?"

- **The patient and loved ones do not need to be entertained or distracted** with anecdotes or jokes, etc. Such talk can be trivializing and offensive. And remember, **talking is no measure of intimacy.** The closest and most comfortable relationships are ones where we can be together in total silence.

A good friend from college called me from Chicago. She was caring for her mother, who was dying of lung cancer. She said, "If I hear one more person tell me some stupid story about their cute kid, I'll scream at them. Why do people think they can distract me with these boring little stories. My mother is dying. I don't care what their little darling did in preschool today!"

- **Remember that some feelings are more socially acceptable than others, and therefore, people in this situation lean on them.** For instance, anger is more acceptable than fear in our society. A patient or caregiver who seems very angry might really be scared and sad.

- **Certain emotional states permeate our family systems; like legacies, they are passed down to our children and grandchildren.** One family expresses sadness with Oscar-winning abandon; another completely squelches the emotion. Some families have members who get angry with one another every single day; others boast, "We haven't had a harsh word in fifteen years of marriage." **We are more open and trusting of those friends who *accept* our family's emotional signature.**

- **Give patients and family members active and direct permission about losing control emotionally.** Keep tissues handy and don't be shy about handing them out. Affirm emotional reactions directly, saying things like, "It's okay to cry. If I were in your shoes, I'd be crying, too." **At a different time, remind them how much they are accomplishing.** (If we compliment them too close to the actual time of the outburst, they will feel we are merely placating them or trying to make them stop being so "emotional.")

- **People differ in their energy levels when it comes to interacting with others.** Some people are energized by company, feeling more alert, more fulfilled when engaged in togetherness activities. Others are exhausted by much contact, restoring their batteries through solitude and individual pursuits. **We close ourselves off to others when we chastise them, even unwittingly, for being our opposites.** The People Person makes a big mistake by judging the Private Person: "He's painfully shy, socially awkward, in fact!" The Private Person makes an error when she judges the People Person: "She's so insecure—she always has to have an audience. Too bad she isn't more comfortable with herself."

- **Some people view their world *logically* and others view their world *emotionally*. In general, it is best to operate within the other person's framework** rather than your own. If we are warm and fuzzy or touchy feely with an analytical person, we'll drive her crazy. If we are all head with a heart person, he'll view us as cold and aloof. **Occasionally, it can be helpful to gently break out of the head or heart mode.** If someone typically expresses what she thinks, we ask also how she feels. When someone typically expresses feelings, we ask also for his thoughts.

- **Sometimes, the very words *thoughts* or *feelings* can be threatening.** In situations where we decide not to be so direct, we can use a more neutral question. "What was your response to that?" can seem less invasive than "How did you feel about that?"

- **As a person approaches death, she sleeps a lot and turns inward,** gathering spiritual strength for this important transition. She expends less energy in here-and-now conversations and interpersonal relationships. During these quiet times, we help most by remaining silent, making her comfortable—also holding her hand, stroking her head, and physically showing her that we are nearby.

- **This sleeping and turning inward can be especially difficult for loved ones; we remember an active, vibrant person who was always laughing, sharing stories, and doing things for others. Family and loved ones often complain or worry about a dying patient's quality of life.** It helps when we can understand that the patient *is* active and indeed her life may be taking on a quality more intense than ever. She *appears* to be sleeping or even coma-tose, but many experts believe she's quite busy sorting through her experiences and readying herself to leave. But since this activity is *internal,* we can't see it in the ways we did before.

- **As mentioned earlier, the patient may now be using symbolic language or she may speak in ways that seem confusing to caretakers.** Often the caretakers say "she's rambling." **This incoherent mind-wandering talk is packed with information, if we listen carefully.** The patient may be using metaphors and other symbolic language to communicate two major things: first, what it feels like to die, and second, what she needs to make a peaceful exit. Helpful loved ones **listen metaphorically and symbolically—not just literally**—and they encourage other family members to do the same.

- **In the closing days of life, many patients have dreams, visions of loved ones who have already died (sometimes hearing their voices beckoning), and powerful—indeed comforting—feelings that they will die soon.** Often, patients are afraid to tell their immediate families and friends about these profound experiences because "it will frighten them, or they'll think I'm hallucinating. Maybe they'll even decide I'm crazy and put me in a nursing home."

- **Loving friends and health care workers are frequently rewarded with hearing these poignant and amazing experiences.** In the happiest families, the closest loved ones get to hear them, too.

14

SILENT SHARING:
THE COMFORTS OF NONVERBAL
COMMUNICATION

These last few weeks have been so different. Mother doesn't care to talk much and she rests a lot. She's always been so opinionated and energetic; it's been a real adjustment. But I sit by her bed and hold her hand, watching over her while she sleeps. She looks very peaceful. And when she comes out of a nap and she sees me there, she smiles with her same old twinkle and gives my hand a squeeze. Then she closes her eyes and falls asleep again. I sometimes sit with her like that for hours.

- **A loved one's smile, his walk, the jutting chin when he's angry—we come to know each other through so much more than words.** When we want to capture the essence of someone, we focus on how she moves, how she smells, how her voice and laughter sound.

- **One reason progressive illness is so difficult—for patients and loved ones alike—is that the patient's nonverbal communication is changing.** He no longer moves like he once did, he can't talk the same way, he doesn't even smell the same.

- **But nonverbal communication is much more than just the physical chemistry between us. Our silent sharing occurs in an environment.** That's why seriously ill people are often so much happier when they can be at home rather than hospitalized. It feels more comfortable to be surrounded by the sights and sounds and smells and objects—people and pets included—we've always known.

- **How we use and define time is another facet of silent sharing.** We feel differently toward the doctor after he glances at a clock during our conversation. Or, we are more anxious when we have to wait until four P.M. for our treatments; we prefer to get them over in the early morning. These effects are not necessarily vocalized, but they do shape our attitudes about our interactions.

- **Time is power.** In any relationship, the person who controls the clock has more power. For instance, it is the parent, not the children, who determines whether siblings can stay up late to visit a loved one at the hospital. It is the *clinic,* not the patient, that determines appointment times and when return phone calls can occur.

- **Incurable people and their loved ones have lost control of the clock.** One moment, they lived with the idea that their futures were more or less infinite. The next moment, they came home from their doctors' offices with parameters. **This can make the patient and loved ones feel powerless.**

- **Those who are not primary caregivers may unintentionally abuse the family's time.** Such people often want to spend time with the patient for their *own* purposes; they may not realize that a seriously ill person has very little energy for interpersonal relationships—even with their mates and closest friends—and especially if death is soon approaching. **Helpful friends can encourage the family to set limits, and they can spread the word among themselves that a ten-minute visit is ample.**

One week I visited a special friend and she was just exhausted. She lived in a retirement high-rise, and friends popped in all the time. She loved the support, she said, but she just wanted to rest more. Right then and there, we took an index card and I printed a nice little message: "Meredith appreciates your love and she also needs to rest. It helps when friends limit a visit to five minutes. Thanks so much." I taped the card to her door, and she gained control over her day.

- **We help the family most when we allow *them* to decide how they spend their time.** Good friends are flexible and take it in stride when the family cancels or reschedules at the very last minute.

- ***Touch* is another essential nonverbal signal; loving friends use tactile communication often and appropriately—with permission.** People with incurable illness are not touched as frequently as they were before; many people are nervous about hurting them, and some even consider disease a stigma. It helps when we brush the patient's hair, massage his hands, hug him, stroke his arm. Of course, **touch is cultural; some cultures are huggers while others prefer to keep a distance.** Be sensitive; helpful friends are loving without overwhelming the family members with affection.

- **People touch in lots of ways. We touch patients clinically, changing dressings, bathing, turning, and feeding. We also touch to provide comfort and compassion through massage, hugging, healing touch.** Sometimes, family members are so exhausted by all the clinical touch that's required, they scarcely have energy to touch the patient for comfort. **Helpful friends perform as many clinical tasks as possible**—such as manicures, hairwashing, pedicures, bathing, changing linens, washing and folding laundry, feeding, cleaning the bath and rest areas. The more clinical tasks friends can do for the family, the more time the family has to spend with the patient providing the luxury of comfort touch.

- **Most patients—and their tired caregivers—greatly appreciate and even crave comfort touch, though they may not ask for it. We can learn to offer it without being asked**—a quick shoulder rub for each family member when we visit, a weekly foot massage and pedicure for the patient. **Providing a clinical function first can ease the sometimes awkward or embarrassing path to comfort touch.** For instance, if we asked a patient, "Would you like a hand massage?" he might feel shy and say, "Oh no, I feel fine, that's okay." Instead, we can say, "Gee, those nails could use a trim," then finish the job with moisturizer (clinical functions), and while applying the lotion, we slip in a relaxing hand massage (for comfort).

- **One of the best times to talk about treacherous topics or scary, sensitive stuff is during a manicure/massage.** The patient and caregiver are close, but we are looking at each other's hands instead of staring into each other's faces. This enhances trust and safety. A vulnerable patient or troubled loved one can struggle with painful emotions and facial expressions in relative privacy even while we are still making physical contact.

- **It helps for *everyone* to be aware of the potential "power trip" in touching others. In any relationship, the person with more power touches the other person more often.** For instance, in a classroom arena, teachers pat their students' shoulders with familiarity, but the student would never be so disrespectful as to return this gesture. Or on the job, the manager congratulates an employee with a hearty pat on the back, but if the employee did this to the boss, she would be considered forward. **A well-meaning friend can overdo a good thing if her touching becomes intrusive.**

- **Eye contact can also be too much of a good thing.** Western European culture teaches us to look people in the eye when we speak to them. But it is important to note that eye contact is culturally determined; many cultures view a direct gaze as a serious sign of disrespect. **And just about everybody needs some private time when face-to-face in conversation.** We help more when we look away occasionally as the person gathers his thoughts or deals with a complex emotion. Give him privacy as he begins to weep. Or we can hold his hands while still looking away. This helps the person feel close to us, but not invaded or exposed.

- **Height is power. We help by getting our head lower than our friend's head, whenever possible.** Use a short stool, sit on the floor beside the couch, lean forward in a chair. Position your face so that you are looking *up* at the person, rather than *down* on her. For example, the best nurses, though much of their work is performed above a patient, usually manage to find sixty seconds or so to crouch by the bed to look up at him, for some gentle conversation.

- **Our *chins* are the most powerful parts of our bodies.** With our chins in the air, we appear arrogant, as if we are "looking down our nose" at the other person. We appear superior, condescending, even confrontational. (Try it in the mirror and see.) To give loved ones more power, it helps when we remember to ever so slightly drop our chins to our chests in each interaction.

- **People who "take up a lot of space" are more powerful, even intimidating** with their big gestures, wide movements, arms akimbo or on hips. We can empower a patient and his loved ones if we tone down our gestures and keep our arms closer to our sides.

- **A pen is a power symbol**—a reflection of the days when our parents shook their fingers at us. Any sort of pointer or extension held in the hands operates as a symbol of authority. We're probably smart to hold the pen when we go for a bank loan; we're better off putting it in our pocket when talking to patients and their loved ones. **This principle also holds true for eyeglasses, rulers, spatulas—or any sort of extension we might unconsciously hold in our hand. It's better to keep our hands open and free of objects when we talk.**

- **A *palms-open* hand position is typically more inviting** than gestures with fists or backs of the hands. When we open our hands to others, we appear much more approachable.

- The posture drawings highlight how we typically pose ourselves to signal power. **Helpful loved ones adopt a submissive posture** to make the patient or family member feel "on top" and more secure.

POWER POSTURES

versus

SUBMISSIVE
(Low Power)

- chin down
- eyes looking up
- arms at sides
- feet inside pelvic area
- taking up less space

DOMINATING
(High Power)

- chin up
- eyes looking down
- arms akimbo
- feet outside pelvic area
- taking up more space
- and for added effect: holding pen or glasses, tapping foot, looking at watch

- **We may not immediately think of the voice as being nonverbal, but our voice is something different and separate from the actual words we speak.** Imagine the simple sentence, "That's a good suggestion!" We can say these very same words in a heartfelt way, in a sarcastic way, in a condescending way, in a surprised way. **Our tone, rate of speech, volume, vocal variety, diction—all can intimidate or invite.** A tentative, softer tone might be more comforting than strong tones with a lot of vocal variety. But if we use a sickeningly sweet tone with a patient or loved one who has a loud or confrontational vocal style, we'll drive him crazy.

- *Up tones* and *Down tones* **are a way of using our voice to reduce defensiveness and manage the conversational flow.** If the last syllable of our sentence goes up in tone, we sound like we are asking a question. If the last syllable goes down in tone, we sound like we are making a statement. For example, say each of these sentences twice, once with an up tone and once with a down tone:

"Would you mind if I came earlier on Fri-*day*?" ↑

"Would you mind if I came earlier on Fri-*day*?" ↓

"The nurse says Peter can't eat solid food any-*more*." ↑

"The nurse says Peter can't eat solid food any-*more*." ↓

- **An up tone sounds tentative, approachable, and inviting. A down tone sounds decisive, powerful, and final. This occurs whether the original sentence was a question or a statement.** If we really *do* want to come earlier on Friday, it helps to ask the question with a down tone, so the response will more likely be yes. But if we need to convey sad news, as in the second example, a down tone can literally feel like a punch in the gut. The news is much softer and easier to hear when delivered with an up tone.

- **Helpful people use up tones to**
  - encourage someone to keep talking
  - soften the blow of bad news
  - make a statement sound like a question

- **Helpful people use down tones to**
  - conclude a conversation
  - predetermine the response to a specific question
  - make a question sound like a statement

- **Supportive friends *mirror* the other person's nonverbal communication.** We match her vocal rhythms, rate of speech, tone, and volume. We match her upright—or slumped—posture. We mirror the slow—or exuberant—gestures. When we adapt to the other person's nonverbal style and preferences, we create extra empathy and trust.

- **We're also aware that different people prefer different amounts of space between them.** Though a standard conversational space between people is about two feet, many people of Middle Eastern descent might like to be much closer, while those of Scandinavian descent might prefer to be farther apart. **Helpful friends allow the other person to set the distance that is most comfortable.**

I've been helping my best friend care for her husband. And her daughter likes to stand so close to me when we talk. It's hard for me to have someone breathing down my neck like that, and it's all I can do to keep from backing away. But she seems to feel more comfortable when I'm close, so I try not to step back.

- **It also helps to learn how to read nonverbal dishonesty.** There are many times during this journey when patients and their loved ones feel they can't tell the entire truth—and for legitimate reasons. Perhaps they don't want to complain, so they tell us everything is fine. Or maybe others become overly anxious or tongue-tied around them, so the family prefers to avert these reactions by saying things are much better than they really are. (See Posturing, p. 35.)

- Some people can just tell when we are hiding our deepest thoughts and feelings. "The truth was written all over her face," they say. "And she couldn't look me in the eye." But **facial expressions and eyes are *not* the best indicators of deception.** We are adept at masking our eyes and facial expressions. We began learning these skills when a parent first said, "You look me in the eye and *then* tell me you didn't eat that licorice I was saving for Grandpa." We were taught to eat foods we hated and to look happy about it. We were coached to smile approvingly at our aunt's new hairstyle, even though the whole family later agreed it was ridiculous. By age five, most of us understood that our eyes and facial expressions had to be controlled if we hoped to "get away with it."

- **We are not so adept at remembering to control other parts of our body.** We might jiggle our feet or curl our toes; we might pull on our nose or cover our mouth when we claim, "Now that Mom has moved in to help take care of Jenny, I'm *much* more relaxed." Or sometimes, we **can't quite synchronize our words with our facial expressions.** For instance, our smile comes *after* our statement instead of during it, because we have to remember to manufacture a smile that can't occur naturally: "The doctors say I'm completely fine. Things couldn't be better." [smile] Or sometimes, **our words contradict our nonverbal behavior.** For example, a caretaking friend looks down and sighs as she tells you that her career isn't suffering.

- **How we touch *ourselves* is another good clue to our true inner state. Such self-touches are unconscious.** We don't really realize we are doing it. Therefore observing these touches can be very helpful in discovering how your loved one really feels. There are three main types:

  - **Soothing Self-Touch**—This occurs when a patient or family member strokes her own arm, hands, hugs herself, or touches herself in other comforting ways when she talks. Soothing self-touch appears when we subconsciously need to calm ourselves, tell ourselves things will be all right, tell ourselves we can make it through an experience (or awkward conversation), etc.

  - **Stimulating Self-Touch**—This occurs when loved ones touch themselves in more erotic but not "taboo" places, such as stroking the neck, thigh, or lips as they speak, or "preening" with the hair or beard. These stimulating self-touches are used when we feel alert, happy, excited, and involved in the conversation, such as when a patient describes a profound dream, or a caretaker tells us about a new relaxation technique he's using.

- **Punishing Self-Touch**—When a caregiver or patient pinches his own arm, bites his thumb, slaps his hands together, pulls at the skin of his neck, or chews his lip, he may be feeling guilty or remorseful about something—for instance, when the caregiver thinks, "I was harsh and impatient," or when the patient feels, "I'm just a burden to the whole family." These touches are often evidence of hiding the truth.

- **Helpful friends can read these self-touches and adapt to them.** We can back off or perhaps gently probe—only *we* can be the judge—when we see self-soothing or punishing behaviors. We can avoid rocking the boat when we see stimulating self-touches. Such signals indicate that we are *already* on a good conversational track.

- **It is also important to understand that these self-touches might not be reflecting the actual conversation we are *currently* having.** Humans commonly conduct conversations while simultaneously thinking about scores of other things. A neck-pinching sister may be privately flashing on an earlier argument she had with her boss, even though we see the gesture when she is speaking about her ill husband. Her self-punishing behavior may not be relevant to her husband at all; it's the unspoken work problem that troubles her. We must try not to jump to conclusions about the meanings of nonverbal behaviors, even when those behaviors appear blatant.

- **Jumping to conclusions is dangerous in any event.** While non-verbal communication *does* account for a major portion of the entire message, it is also highly subjective, culturally determined, and easy to misread. When assessing a loved one's motivations or unspoken thoughts and feelings, it is essential look for corroborating evidence. We need to use more than one nonverbal cue and also to listen to verbal messages, when drawing conclusions.

- *An important point:* **Just because we see evidence of nonverbal deception *doesn't* mean we ought to automatically draw attention to it—and especially *not* at the specific moment the be-**

havior occurs. If patients and their loved ones feel the need to alter the spin of their circumstances at a given moment, it's often more helpful to let them. *Later* you might decide to talk about it—or not.

NOTES

15

MANAGING FAMILY CONFLICT

- **It helps to remind ourselves, and to gently remind our loved ones, that venting and anger are normal** under any circumstances. With the family experiencing the additional stresses of serious illness, people are especially likely to be edgy. Conflicts may erupt. **Conflict can actually be a *helpful* communication dynamic,** since it forces us to view more than one perspective of the situation. Of course, we have to be willing to do this, first. **Managing conflict takes energy.** We have to control emotions, listen well, and weigh words carefully. If managing conflict is a mountain, the higher we climb toward resolving our problems, the greater the effort required.

- **Managing conflict is complicated by the fact that different loved ones are at different stages of acceptance** regarding the family's situation. For example, an incurable man wants to discuss his estate with a daughter who denies that her father is seriously ill. She wants to *ignore* the issues while he wants to *confront* them.

- **There is a *cost* and *reward* in choosing any communication behavior, but particularly in managing conflict.** We weigh the potential cost against the reward and decide if our conversations will be worth it; will we be able to resolve the issues? Will we be able to overcome the other person's resistance? We decide that some issues are just not worth our energy. With others, it seems essential to lay our cards on the table. **It would be easier if everyone agreed on the relative rewards and costs of having a given discussion. Unfortunately, this is rarely the case.** Therefore, our *first* discussion is often "whether or not we'll even *address* this conflict."

- **Our personality styles predispose us to vastly different approaches to conflict. One family member has a "fight"**

approach when faced with serious illness, another prefers to "take flight." The first says, "Let's pick up the phone right now and talk to the doctor about this new rash." The other answers, "Can't we just try to *enjoy* ourselves for once and rent a movie? It's just dry skin. We see the nurse next week—let's talk then." The first then argues, "You're avoiding this." The second retorts, "I am *not*. *You're* overreacting, just making a mountain out of a molehill."

- **People in close relationships (husband and wife, mother and son) often have opposite preferences. Theirs is a complementary fight-flight approach.** Punctuated by periods of calm and storm, these are the relationships that will be subject to disagreements about *whether* there should be any discussion at all. **Or sometimes, two fighters are in a primary relationship.** Theirs is a loud, confrontational fight-fight method of handling conflict. They are energized by argument, and they seem to fight about everything. Sometimes this fight mode permeates the whole family; the entire household seems volatile and expressive. **Finally, both parties might be flight takers.** Their relationship appears calm, but privately, unspoken conflict still exists. The flight pattern can also extend throughout the entire family; the household is quiet and guarded. **No method is better; they are just different.**

- **Any person who feels anger or conflict will behave defensively.** It is difficult to monitor our behaviors and be tactful and sensitive when emotions are at a fevered pitch.

- **There is no need to apologize for feeling defensive.** *Any* time we feel challenged, scared, or anxious, we pull back or strike out to protect ourselves. And certainly, serious illness contains all these ingredients—in a very major way.

- **Defensiveness is normal, even helpful.** We can think of our various defense mechanisms as a crutch, a tool that is temporarily necessary to help us through some especially rough terrain. We mustn't try to get rid of this crutch. Instead, we tolerate it, with the knowledge that our hurts *will* heal, and eventually the crutch won't be necessary.

- **When a loved one shouts, "You're so *defensive!*" a response like "No, I'm *not!*" only escalates emotions and pulls us away from the real issues.** Suddenly, we are arguing about our reactions to the problem, not the problem itself. **A much more effective response to this "attack" is to acknowledge it:** "You're right. I *do* feel defensive. I'm scared and angry, and it's hard for me to think and speak clearly right now."

- **Rather than denying each other's right to be defensive, helpful loved ones learn to acknowledge and recognize the specific *ways* we become defensive**—and we examine our own defensive behaviors more often than we point out these behaviors in others.

- **There are a number of defensive postures:**

    THE RATIONALIZER: Finding reasons to justify an unhappy turn of events.

    "It's actually okay that my father is dying; he's old enough to have had a full and happy life."

    Helpful response: Do not discount the explanations/logic of the person, regardless how crazy or preposterous they seem. "It's *okay* that your father is dying?! Oh, come *on* now!" This will only make the person explain even more. Instead, just listen, nod, and be careful not to smile (which this person would certainly find patronizing).

    THE OSTRICH: Totally suppressing any feelings of defeat/anger/pain/failure. Danger lies in the fact that repressed feelings explode, eventually.

    "Tina always seemed to be so cheerful and bright, until I found her sobbing hysterically in front of the TV last night. The sound wasn't even turned on. I was really scared; she was the one who was keeping me in control."

Helpful response: Do not try to force the "ostrich" to talk. "Tina, you're in denial—it's so *obvious.* You'll feel so much better if you just *talk* about this." No, she won't, and if we confront her this directly, she'll squirm and probably wish she could run from the room. If we feel we *must* get her to open up, we can try asking very neutral, nonthreatening questions: "So, what were the best and worst parts of your day today?"

THE FINGER POINTER: Blaming someone else to explain our own fears or failures.

"How can I be expected to put together a decent meal for everyone when I have to spend half the afternoon chasing after your father's prescription?"

Helpful response: Do not try to get the person to admit her fears or failures. "Come on now, no one is looking for a gourmet meal, and besides, the pharmacy is only ten minutes away." This only makes the person deny responsibility even more vehemently. Instead say, "It isn't really important how this happened—let's just solve the problem. How about if we order a pizza?"

THE COMPENSATOR: Treating ourselves when things are difficult, threatening, etc. This is a basis for serious problems like obesity, bankruptcy, and chemical dependency.

"The only way I can get through my evening visit to the hospital is to pop over to the mall afterwards. I've bought three pairs of shoes this month."

Helpful response: Do not call attention to the treats. This will not eliminate them; it will only cause the person to hide them. (Obviously in severe cases such as bingeing, massive debt, or drug dependency, intervention is sometimes necessary.)

THE PROTESTER: Publicly taking a position that is the opp
of what we privately feel, because we think our private thoug.
are wrong or taboo.

> *"Why should anyone be afraid of dying? We've always believed that God has a better future in store for us!"*

Helpful response: Like the Rationalizer, this person will only become more defensive if we point out inconsistencies and illogical statements. Avoid arguing and don't focus on what was said; let the statements slide.

THE REACTOR: Taking out anger or frustrations on something unrelated to the conflict—hopefully an inanimate object, but not always.

> *"Boy, Rita was really slamming the dishes around last night!"*

Helpful response: Do not tell the person to calm down. This will only infuriate her even more. Instead, get out of the way! Later, calmly acknowledge apologies and try not to make her feel any more guilty about damage that was done. Allow her some private time to clean up, repair, and replace. (Obviously in severe cases of physical/verbal abuse, intervention is in order.)

- **Above all, it's wise to avoid immediately arguing with a defensive person.** Contradicting him will make him even more defensive. Instead, **give him plenty of time to vent.** Use nods and um-hmms (minimal encouragers). This lets you participate without talking too much. At first, ask easy probing questions. Later, and *only once he's ready* to analyze instead of emote, try paraphrase—your playback of his ideas will help him clarify and calm down. Be careful to avoid any tone of "I told you so." (See Listening and Responding with All Our Senses , p. 91.)

- **We're also careful to adopt a nonverbal style that invites rather than intimidates.** (See Silent Sharing, p. 107.)

- **Another helpful tool is a tangible list of ground rules for communicating during conflict.** When emotions run rampant we

THE PROTESTER: Publicly taking a position that is the opposite of what we privately feel, because we think our private thoughts are wrong or taboo.

"Why should anyone be afraid of dying? We've always believed that God has a better future in store for us!"

Helpful response: Like the Rationalizer, this person will only become more defensive if we point out inconsistencies and illogical statements. Avoid arguing and don't focus on what was said; let the statements slide.

THE REACTOR: Taking out anger or frustrations on something unrelated to the conflict—hopefully an inanimate object, but not always.

"Boy, Rita was really slamming the dishes around last night!"

Helpful response: Do not tell the person to calm down. This will only infuriate her even more. Instead, get out of the way! Later, calmly acknowledge apologies and try not to make her feel any more guilty about damage that was done. Allow her some private time to clean up, repair, and replace. (Obviously in severe cases of physical/verbal abuse, intervention is in order.)

- **Above all, it's wise to avoid immediately arguing with a defensive person.** Contradicting him will make him even more defensive. Instead, **give him plenty of time to vent.** Use nods and um-hmms (minimal encouragers). This lets you participate without talking too much. At first, ask easy probing questions. Later, and *only once he's ready* to analyze instead of emote, try paraphrase—your playback of his ideas will help him clarify and calm down. Be careful to avoid any tone of "I told you so." (See Listening and Responding with All Our Senses , p. 91.)

- **We're also careful to adopt a nonverbal style that invites rather than intimidates.** (See Silent Sharing, p. 107.)

- **Another helpful tool is a tangible list of ground rules for communicating during conflict.** When emotions run rampant we keep each other on track by gently enforcing rules like the ones at the end of this chapter. And it's wisest to correct *ourselves* before correcting others. Custom-tailor this list to fit your own family style. For instance, is profanity okay? sarcasm? **Refine the rules together, then make an actual copy, and place the page on the coffee table between the communicators.** When a rule is being broken, merely point to an item rather than saying something, and avoid being self-righteous about it; this can reduce ego damage and silly arguments.

• **Some family conflicts are impossible to resolve without objective, outside help. What this family needs is a *mediator*—** a professional trained in conflict resolution who listens to all parties, ensures that they listen to each other, and suggests methods for finding solutions. A mediator *does not* come up with the solutions herself and impose them on the parties; family members still have total control over their own problems. Fees are generally determined on ability to pay; in some areas, a family can even find mediation services for free. **Look in the Yellow Pages under Mediation** for agency names and phone numbers.

• **But before you get to this point, make time to take a breather: do something fun as a family.** Forget about the issues for a day or two. Afterward, schedule a creativity meeting to toss around new ideas—rejuvenate, and get back on track. For help with this kind of problem solving, please turn to the next chapter.

GROUND RULES FOR COMMUNICATING DURING CONFLICT

1. **Make "I" statements.** Talk about your own perspective and experience, not theirs. For example, "I worked very hard to make these weekend arrangements for Dad" instead of "You don't appreciate me."

2. **Avoid words that evoke defensiveness** (*you, always, never, should, why,* or "loaded" terms). When a unique term (like

NOTES

16

SOLVING PROBLEMS
THE CREATIVE WAY

- **The crisis of illness motivates families to do some creative problem solving.** It's best when conflicts can be negotiated creatively, and decisions concerning a loved one are made with care.

- **Solving problems requires two very different brain activities and both are vital to the process.**

  - Right Brain: generating of ideas, new information, possible solutions

  - Left Brain: assessing of those ideas, evaluating and choosing the best alternative

PROBLEM SOLVING

CREATIVITY *(Step One)*	DECISION-MAKING *(Step Two)*
Generate Ideas/Info	Assess Ideas/Info
Right Brain	Left Brain
Subjective	Objective
Emotional/Feelings	Logical/Thoughts
Intuitive	Analytical
Spatial	Linear
Unstructured	Structured
Random	Sequential
Unlimited	Limited
Open-Ended	Close-Ended
Fuzzy	Focused
Process Oriented	Outcome Oriented
Broad	Narrow
Nonevaluative	Evaluative

- **Most of us fail to separate these two steps.** Instead, we blend them, trying to perform them simultaneously. We assess ideas just at the moment we are trying to generate them. *Nothing will stymie us faster.* Family members sometimes combine creativity with decision-making in the mistaken belief that it saves time. "Let's just toss out a few ideas about Mom's situation and figure out the best one. And let's get going—we need a *decision.* We can't just sit on this problem forever." **This shortsighted approach sabotages the gathering of new ideas. In the long run, it *wastes* time.**

My brother Frank was so bossy when we were deciding how we could care for Dad. He arrived at our family meeting with these four ideas on a clipboard—he's the oldest, also an accountant—you get the picture. So we all spent an hour talking about his four plans, basically trashing them, because no one else liked them. Finally, my sister-in-law Nancy said, "You know, Frank, those four aren't the only options we have." Then she told us to go around the room and shout out ideas real fast, and she'd write them all down. The wilder and crazier the better, she said, and we weren't allowed to discuss any of them yet. We called out ideas for about fifteen minutes and we had pages of stuff to work with. Plus we were laughing and really having fun. Some of the ideas were pretty silly, like when Timmy said, "I think Grandpa should stay in the bathtub." But later, even that led us to realize Dad could have his baths at the daycare center where he goes three times a week. They have lots of home health aides there, and now that's one less job for us. We should have started with Nancy's brainstorming thing in the first place. It would have saved a lot of time.

- **Making decisions requires negotiation, but sadly, we are conditioned all our lives to use win-lose tactics.** We've been taught from age zero to look out for number one. In a sense we have to start over; we need to retrain ourselves to negotiate in new ways.

- **Most people define win-win negotiation like so: "It's when each party is willing to bend a little,** each person is willing to give in on something—no one is greedy or tries to take it all." Actually, this is *not* win-win negotiation. Those words define *compromise,* also known as lose-lose. The inherent belief in compromise is that there isn't enough to go around; we have to divvy up our limited resources.

- **A win-win approach considers resources to be *abundant* rather than *scarce.*** Our possibilities are viewed as endless. There are many ways to solve our problems. It's just that we need to discover them. And there are other important differences between these approaches:

WIN-LOSE NEGOTIATING VS. WIN-WIN NEGOTIATING

SCARCITY BELIEFS: *"There isn't enough family around to care for Mom."*	ABUNDANCE BELIEFS: *"Mom also has lots of friends and even acquaintances who could help."*
OUTCOME ORIENTED: *"If we involve her in this decision, we'll never be able to move her into a nursing home."*	PROCESS ORIENTED: *"She needs a voice in how she's cared for, too, even if that means we have to think of a different solution or it takes longer."*
SHORT-TERM GAIN: *"She can't understand what's happening anyway—what's the difference? This is easier."*	LONG-TERM GAIN: *"We'll all feel better about this in the future, if we don't push her to do something she doesn't want to do right now."*
GREED: *"I refuse to give up my weekends to take care of her. It's the only time Paul and I have together."*	NEED: *"Maybe I can do weekends, and even bring your kids so you and Paul can really get away. I'm more worried about the weeknights when I have to work."*
HIDE INFORMATION: *"I'm not sure of my work schedule. I never find out until right before."*	SHARE INFORMATION: *"Here are the nights I have to work in the next few weeks."*

- **Win-win negotiating is far more humane and loving. It also** *takes more time.* We need patience when trying to discover each other's needs. We must be willing to persist when looking for more ideas when solutions don't satisfy everyone. In short, we sometimes get frustrated but we *don't give up.*

- *Attitude* **is the most important attribute of any successful win-win negotiation.** We need a can-do approach, and we need faith that everyone can be satisfied. We also need to believe that human beings are basically good and ethical. The best way for us to "walk our talk" about the goodness of others is to be a good person ourselves, and to **carefully sidestep those tricks and strategies that are so damaging to win-win relationships.**

- **Work hard to avoid these destructive behaviors:**

  - **"Nibbling" for more concessions after the main deal has been decided.** *"Since you're okay with taking Jerry to the doctor, it really wouldn't be out of your way to go to the grocery store, too."*

  - **"Playing chicken" by issuing an ultimatum and hoping the other person is scared into complying.** *"If you won't move back home to help me take care of your father, I'm going to have to put him in a nursing home."*

  - **"Playing highball-lowball" by making a ridiculously high (or low) opening offer.** *"I'm willing to take care of Dad, but I think each of my brothers' families ought to pay me $1,000 a month to do it."*

  - **Good-guy/bad-guy tactics, wherein the people you are negotiating with suddenly have partners; one is nice and befriends you, the other attacks you.** The nice one protects you from the mean one. These tactics are quite common in family negotiations. *"Buddy is just furious because you forgot Nancy's prescription. He didn't realize until ten o'clock last night; he had to go out to get it. I told him I'd go, but he just stomped out the door. When he got back I tried to remind him how busy you are, but he just kept shouting about dependability. I finally calmed him down by telling him you'd come over all day Saturday to do whatever chores he needs done. You* will *be there, I trust!!"*

- **Deliberate use of anger** where we pretend to be very angry. We stomp out of the room, have an angry outburst, all in the interest of intimidating the other person into complying.

- **Beefing up our position officially, making things appear legitimate** by setting up policies, procedures, presenting contracts and written outlines of meeting agendas, etc. *"We're having this family meeting with the hospice nurse when Julie waltzes in with a clipboard. She hands everyone an outline and says, 'These are the questions I want the hospice program to address. I'm sure the rest of you have others. Let's start with number one.' Little Miss Efficiency. She thinks she's our fearless leader, so she just moved right in and took over the meeting."*

- **The "Columbo" effect, *acting* confused, acting powerless,** so that others will think you are harmless and share secrets that could ultimately be used against them. *"You don't know where Dad put his important papers? But before he got so sick, I thought he made you executor of the estate!"*

- **Scorekeeping, keeping a verbal or even written tally** of each person's concessions and compromises, bringing up past wrongs, operating in a tit-for-tat manner. *"I've changed Mom's bedding the last three times. Plus I've made dinner more often than you have. You should give Mom her bath."*

- **Stalling, putting you off, not making a decision when you want one,** "forgetting" deadlines or commitments, a form of power-tripping over you. *"I know I told you I'd talk to Mary about taking Dad for the holidays, but I just didn't have enough time. I won't be able to give you an answer for a few more days."*

- **Denying authority,** informing the person needing a decision that, contrary to what they thought, *you* are not authorized to make a decision, sometimes making that "other" decision-maker hard to reach. *"I agree that Mom would be helped by a nurse's aide, but my brother has the final say. I'll talk to him, but I can't promise anything. No, don't bother to call him. You'd only get his voice mail anyway."*

- **Helpful friends and loved ones are committed to pulling themselves out of such competitive and destructive behaviors.** We gently remind each other when a win-win principle is being ignored. And most important, we strive to improve our *own* behavior before trying to fix everyone else's.

- **It is also important to remember that any negotiation is drastically affected by its *audience*.** Most negotiations don't happen in a vacuum. Their outcome affects lots of people besides the negotiators. Consider these effects of audience:

  - Is the family alone when making decisions or are others present (friends, medical professionals, shirttail relatives)?

  - How often do the various family members see each other?

  - Among friends and family, what is their degree of involvement in this illness? in other areas of your life, besides this illness?

  - Are these involved people directly or indirectly connected to the *specific* negotiation at hand (about living arrangements, finances, transportation to doctors' appointments)?

  - What kind of feedback are they giving the negotiators, if any?

  - What is their specific relationship to the negotiator—legal ties, emotional ties, blood ties, history of relationship?

  - What is the audience's role in this negotiation, and their willingness or desire to affect its outcome?

- **Research shows that an audience usually makes two negotiators much *more* win-lose and competitive** in nature. When we negotiate in front of others, we want to prove to our *own* "team" just how tough we can be. "I'm strong, I won't be pushed around, I'll make sure *my* family doesn't get screwed here." **Helpful friends and loved ones realize that an audience can make negotiators bloodthirsty.** They make a big effort to stay away from the arena during decision-making that doesn't immediately affect them.

- **It also helps when family and friends appoint an actual *Chairperson*** for a specific decision-making session, including sessions devoted to creativity and generating new ideas. This person keeps the group orderly and ensures that all available information will be considered, even the perspectives of a child. He or she acts as emcee during discussions, voting, and so on.

- **The family and loved ones need to be conscious of the methods used to make their ultimate decisions.** For instance, imagine the family is considering hospice for a loved one with dementia. Who is eligible to vote? Do the children have a say? Does the group need a majority? Do they prefer a unanimous consensus? Or is the decision a dictatorial one? Whatever the rules, the circle of loved ones needs to understand how their decision-making affects their family dynamics.

- **It also helps to know that we are more prone to accept and comply with a decision if we have a voice in shaping it.** Even if your ill brother moving in with you is a given, how the family rearranges its living space is best decided with your kids and spouse.

- **When the time comes for the circle of loved ones to make decisions, it's wisest to look at their lists of ideas and highlight the positive ones,** rather than talking about the bad ideas and why they won't work.

- **The more a family understands its own conflict, negotiation, and decision-making styles and habits, the better.** We need to learn to dance with each other, even though some prefer to waltz and others like slam dancing. We adapt to new methods; we listen to unusual music. It's best to concentrate on each step and its intricacies, not just the end result or how much we step on each other's toes.

Before this happens to you, you never imagine you'll be making so many decisions and juggling so many details and trying to keep so many people happy. It's exhausting.

*We had to discuss everything. And I mean, every last thing.
We went back and forth with the doctors, the nurses, the social
worker. With each other. We went home to our own families and
went back and forth some more with them. From big things like
"Should Mom go into hospice" to medium things like "Who's going to live with Mom this week" to tiny things like "Who's going
to take Mom to the doctor," You name it, we discussed it. I feel
like I spent the last year getting a Ph.D. in family conflict.*

• Once a family can work well together when negotiating and making decisions, they are more prone to play well together, too. And
this is the fun part about solving problems—coming up with
original ideas and creative alternatives. **To gather ideas that offer real solutions, set the scene for play and creativity.** The
atmosphere *will* affect our moods, so work to enhance it.

  • **Choose a comfortable environment.** Pay attention to light-
  ing, seating, work surface. Play soft, easy-listening music. Turn
  off the TV. Turn *on* the answering machine. Offer refresh-
  ments. Share lots of laughter.

  • **Attitude is also atmosphere,** not just the physical environment. Encourage silliness and childlike inhibition.

  • **To adjust attitude, spend two to five minutes doing a group
  relaxation exercise** such as stretching, meditating, storytell-
  ing, drawing, playing catch with a piece of paper. Start the
  session by doing something together that separates this time
  from where you were as individuals, before.

  • **Suspend all judgment.** For the next fifteen minutes no one
  is allowed to say anything that evaluates, either negatively or
  positively. For example, they cannot say, "That won't work"
  and they cannot say, "That's a great idea." Gently but firmly
  enforce the rule, throughout the session. Work to correct
  yourself before correcting others.

  • **Go for quantity, not quality.** It doesn't matter if the ideas are
  ridiculous. The group's game is to generate the greatest num-

ber in the shortest amount of time. (You'll evaluate them all later. For now, just spit 'em out!)

- **Go for crazy, not sane.** The more frivolous and freewheeling your thinking, the better. The wilder your ideas and attitudes, the better.

- **Use all five senses,** and especially choose those that are used the least. Describe the situation in terms of its smell, taste, and texture instead of just its scene or sound. Trust the sixth sense—intuition—too.

- **Change routines—radically.** Hold the brainstorming session at midnight or at the zoo or at the science museum. Do the brainstorming on huge sheets of brown kraft paper in Magic Markers. Have hamburgers and fries for breakfast during your session. Wear unusual clothing. In short, break free from subtle and self-imposed restrictions and inhibitions.

- **Instead of "Why not" ask "What if."**

- **We must ban negativity and avoid statements like**

"But . . ."   *"Why would you want to do*
"That's not logical."   *that?"*
"Don't be foolish."   *"That's not my responsibility."*
"That's already been tried."   *"This is just frivolous and silly."*
"Someone will make a mis-   *"I have no idea how to help."*
take."   *"I'm just not creative."*

- **We need to feel free to** *experiment*—**to try something new for a brief time**—**and remind ourselves that it is okay to change directions.** No idea is the only idea; no plan is the only plan. For instance, when the family needs to change a living arrangement or alter a diet, say, "How about trying this for a few days. If it doesn't work, we'll figure out something new to try."

- Here are some specific **methods for generating ideas.** Choose a few to try at your next family discussion. As your circle practices them, **work toward establishing trust.** Once your loved ones realize they won't be laughed at, criticized, or made to feel foolish, their creativity will flourish.

METHODS FOR GENERATING IDEAS

• **Brainstorm.** This is the most widely used technique for generating new ideas. It isn't always performed properly, however. Lots of people make the mistake of giving positive feedback when there ought to be no judgment at all. (A comment like "That's a wonderful idea!" keeps the group focused on *that* idea, instead of thinking of numerous others.) Directions: Set aside five–fifteen minutes to consider your issue and list everything that comes to mind. Go around the small group and call out ideas, the crazier the better. The major rule is *no evaluation*. Choose a scribe to record all ideas. Two scribes (each writing down every other idea that gets called out) can make the process even more efficient. The goal is to come up with as many ideas as possible within the space of a few minutes. Later you will take this list and use it to refine your solutions and choose among them.

• **Go outside the problem.** Remind one another that resources are infinite; force yourselves to go outside your normal boundaries. (For instance, it isn't just *relatives* that could care for your father; his best friend from high school is also a possibility.) Make it a game to come up with the most unusual suggestions. Or mentally place yourselves in a foreign country solving this problem. What would your priorities be if you lived in Mexico, and had this illness? Or to get your imaginations going, ask yourselves, "What if we lived under water (or in outer space) and had to care for Grandpa? How would we solve our problems then?" You might be amazed at the number of ideas you derive for this weird situation that truly apply to the real one the family wants to resolve.

• **Free-write.** Free-writing exercises can be performed alone or in groups. Set the kitchen timer for two–five minutes. Each person individually writes about the issue. The only rule: your pen must write continuously and you cannot stop writing until the time is up. If you can't think of what to write, just write "I can't think of what to write, I can't think of—" and soon you'll be back on track. After the time is up, each person silently reads what's on the paper and has the option of sharing it aloud. Try free-writing for a family whose ideas seem to have stagnated. It is also helpful when tensions are high, so that the family can vent without saying hurtful things they'll later regret. (See Therapies for Stress and Burnout, p. 139.)

• **Group-write.** Loved ones are passed a pad of paper and instructed to write about the situation. Every two minutes the pad gets passed to another member who continues writing the story where the last one left off. Pass the pad around to each member several times. After about thirty minutes (during which time everyone who isn't writing enjoys chatting over snacks), the entire group gathers together and chooses someone to read aloud the entire document. This is a great exercise for generating discussion, creating new ideas, seeing lots of alternative perspectives, and creating a strong bond within the group of loved ones. It's fun and only takes an hour.

• **Think in spatial rather than linear terms.** Most of us are used to outlining our ideas in Roman numeral fashion. We've been doing it since fourth-grade composition class. Help friends and loved ones see the situation in visual or metaphorical ways, instead of linear sentences. For instance, have them talk about the illness as a safari or a volcano. What new ideas can be sparked by this new visual perspective?

• **Mind-mapping** is another nonlinear method of drawing our ideas instead of outlining them in words. This technique can really help put a fresh spin on the same old situation, and it's a lot of fun. It only takes thirty minutes or so, a worthwhile investment. Directions: Mind-mapping is best with lots of colors and plenty of room, so gather the markers and keep kraft paper or newsprint handy. Gather the family and give each a large sheet of paper. Instruct them to doodle about the situation. Instead of limiting themselves to words, encourage them to express themselves with symbols, logos, bridges, arrows, rainbows, whatever strikes the fancy. After about fifteen minutes, have each family member hold up their mind map to tell about it—the connections, the metaphors, the colors. A variation: use a really large piece of paper and gather several loved ones around it. Perhaps use the dining room table. The entire group mind-maps on the same piece of paper—joining their pictures or not, whatever seems appropriate. Another variation: Ban the use of words entirely. Make everyone draw the situation, exclusively.

• **Listen to kids.** Kids are free thinking and soaring, which is how we *all* started out, before we found ourselves boxed in by responsibilities and practical concerns. To remind yourself of a kid's creative powers, try a simple exercise. Draw a dot on a piece of paper. Ask an adult, "What is this?" Then ask the question again to someone younger than 6. Compare the responses.

Marcie always did the cooking for our family. Maybe it sounds silly, but when she got sick, dinnertime became the most stressful part of my day. I can't stand trying to come up with dinner, night after night, for four cranky, picky-eater kids. One day I was staring into the open fridge, and my six-year-old, Ben, walked up. "What's wrong, Dad?" he asked. I told him I couldn't think of what to make for dinner. He looked in the fridge and quickly pulled out a few ingredients—cottage cheese, turkey, and grated cheese. "Everyone loves all of these things. Here, just cut up the turkey and mix everything together in a big bowl. And make some frozen peas to keep Mom happy. It will be delicious."

It was, too. It wasn't the most beautiful entree you ever saw, but it sure was tasty. Not a single gripe, either.

Now I rarely stand at an open fridge. I save myself a ton of trouble by just calling out, "Hey, Ben!"

17

THERAPIES FOR
STRESS AND BURNOUT

- **A therapy is anything that interrupts stress, reduces discomfort, and attends to the physical, mental, and spiritual needs of both patients and caregivers.** Below is a brief overview of many different therapies for patients and their loved ones.

WRITING

- **Writing enables us to explain things, express our feelings, and escape. It is also physical *work*.** Many patients lack the stamina to hold pen to paper (or to keyboard) for long. Talking into a small, inexpensive tape player is another way to accomplish the same goal.

- **A helpful gesture is to offer to be the patient's "pen" to write letters (see below) and record feelings or dreams.** The right person can be the pen for private writing, too, such as very personal journals, logs, or memoirs.

- **For the patient, it's good therapy to write letters to people we love and know,** even to people who are no longer living. Write letters that we will mail, write others that we will not. Write letters to people who have hurt, disappointed, or angered us. This therapy is especially useful for coming to terms with irreconcilable conflicts. **Write a legacy letter to each of the friends and family members we love,** telling them specifically what they mean to us, what memories we have of them, or what we wish for them in their futures.

- **Free-write. This technique gets the creative juices going, and it also makes a great tool for venting.** If you can't think what to write, just write that until you think of something. When you're finished, read back what you wrote. Maybe it makes sense, maybe it's funny, but you'll definitely be more clearheaded.

- **Keep a journal of experiences, thoughts, and feelings,** as a caregiver or as a patient. If you need help, buy a book on journal writing to get you started. **Find fantasy through writing,** to explain and escape. Create characters, situations, and images that express what is happening to you and your family. **Write essays and editorials about your specific illness.** Or, **write essays and articles about things other than the illness**—like politics, gardening, remodeling. Choose a favorite cause or interest and "make a mark."

READING

- **Reading, like writing, requires physical energy. Many patients may not have the stamina to hold up a book for very long.** Offer to read to them and make weekly trips to the library for books on tape.

- **Read books and articles about the patient's specific condition, concerns, issues.** Family counselors call this technique bibliotherapy. It means "reading about your problems and possible solutions."

TOUCH

- **Massage is one of the best therapies around—both in the giving and the getting.** Caregivers ought to seriously consider finding a good therapist and making a monthly or biweekly appointment. This may cost forty to eighty dollars per visit—and don't even bother with anything less than an hour-long, full-body massage—but you'll feel wonderful afterward. And looking forward to your next regular visit can pull you through some mighty stressful times. **Providing the funds for regular massage therapy is a wonderful gift for friends to give a primary caregiver.**

- **When money is tight, we can always train *ourselves* in massage techniques.** There are many wonderful, easy-reading books in the library on the best methods for massaging. **And remember, a partner isn't necessary. You can always massage yourself—at least partially.** Bathe your feet, turn on a cozy lamp, put on some quiet music. Grab a towel and lotion and give your feet and calves a nice long rub.

- **It's surely obvious that many patients have health restrictions that prohibit a deep full-body massage.** Certain body areas might have internal tumors, pains, or protrusions not visible to the eye. Other sections might be visibly changed due to the illness, causing the patient embarrassment. Areas of skin might have lesions or be weakened so that pressured rubbing is uncomfortable, not to mention unadvisable. Ask your ill friend or loved one what feels best, be sensitive about avoiding painful or embarrassing areas, and start light and gentle versus deep and penetrating.

- Full-body massage takes time and energy—**perhaps you can give a partial massage, instead.** Don't automatically jump to the back or the neck! Different people carry their tension in different parts of their bodies. Some people will especially prefer a leg massage. Others, a head, face, feet, or hands massage.

EXERCISE

- **Everyone knows the benefits of exercising; too many of us make excuses to fall out of a regular routine. It is especially easy for patients and caregivers to come up with excuses.** "I'm too weak." "I get enough exercise just lifting and caring for my husband." "I just don't have the energy for that." "I'd love to go for a walk every day, but who would look after my mother?" Remind yourself of all the studies that show that stress, fatigue, and depression are relieved by exercise. Make a commitment to take care of yourself. Reach out to friends and ask for respite so you can go for a walk four times a week.

- **Patients need regular exercise, too, but the "therapy" of it all can become murky.** We often think of caretakers as doing too much for the patient, refusing the patient enough exercise or independence. But more commonly, the opposite mistake is made—**primary caregivers tend to force a patient to take on much *more* exercise than she wants or needs.**

- **Therapeutic exercise for seriously ill people does not mean a long walk around the block.** Rather, it means moving from the bed to a chair to watch kids in the playground across the street, or walking into the den to sit at the desk and look over old photographs. Or getting bundled into the car to go for a drive through a favorite park. **Friends, family, and caregivers must work hard to appreciate and accept the patient's new limitations.** Never let your loved one forget that he is much more than his physical body, which sometimes seems to let him down in new ways, every day.

- **Caretaking family members and loved ones need to ask themselves,** "Do I really want her to be more active for *her* sake? Or for *mine?*"

Lots of times, my hospice patients struggle so much physically, and their caregiver seems to just pile it on even more. I remember one woman—she was very young and it was hard for her husband to accept that she was so ill. He made her do everything. She could barely manage to lift up her spoon anymore, but he made her feed herself even if it took forty-five minutes.

One time with her, it was just a few weeks before she died, she needed to get to the bathroom. We were in the living room—just 15 feet from the downstairs bathroom she used. I said, "Do you want to use your chair?" and she said yes. Her husband was in the kitchen and saw us, and he called out, "Dorothy, you can walk that!" I was holding her by the shoulders when he said it, and I felt her body just deflate with despair, literally. She was so tired by this time. I said quietly, "Let me just get your chair," and she said, "No, I'll walk."

So, we walked. It took about ten minutes to get there, seriously. She had to stop to catch her breath with every single step. And during the middle of it all, we both realized how hard it was becoming. But I couldn't let go now, because her chair was too far away and she was so weak she might fall. I said, "Let me ask Paul to get your chair for us." She said, "NO!" really emphatically. By the time I finally had her safely propped up at the bathroom sink, I said, "That was a little harder than we thought it would be." She said, "That's okay. It makes Paul feel better—and it keeps him off my back."

I drove home from that visit really sad. Here she was so tired. . . . She could have used every gentle twenty minutes available by that point. But she had to waste her precious energy doing a stupid thing like getting to the bathroom. And why? Because he couldn't accept that she was weak and needed the chair.

RETREAT

- **Travel is one form of retreat,** by ourselves, with a friend, or with an intimate loved one. It can be exotic and elaborate, like fulfilling the dream of a trip to Europe. Or, it can be as simple as checking into a local hotel for a night. Order room service. Swim. Watch movies all night long. Go alone, with a spouse, with a best friend. Sit up and gab or pull the covers over your heads and sleep for twelve hours straight.

- **For long-term caregivers, it's a good idea to take lots of overnight retreats to local hotels — once a month, if possible. Caregivers ought to consider taking a true vacation once or twice a year, in addition.** This could add up to a budget already stretched with medical expenses. Such getaways are thoughtful gifts for groups of friends to give.

- **Be creative in figuring out ways to pool financial resources to help families dealing with incurable illness.** Perhaps there are ten or more adults in your circle who could contribute thirty to fifty dollars per year to a Caregivers' Annual Vacation Fund. Or maybe you could host a fund-raising lasagna dinner for your caregiving loved one and a bon voyage party.

• **Make it a practice to hire a home health aide or nurse to care for the patient or put another trusted family member in charge,** just for a few days out of every year—and take off.

• **Many families who live with incurable illness are extremely enthusiastic about retreats they've taken with other families who share similar problems.** Organizations throughout the nation are now sponsoring camps and conferences, custom-tailored to families with specific diseases. To discover what might be available in your area, call hotlines and national organizations that provide information for people with a specific disease.

MUSIC

• **Research into the benefits of music therapy for incurable people is relatively new, but indications are that music can operate as a *pain-relieving* agent.** Classical or new-age music can promote muscle relaxation and relieve anxiety and depression, thus altering the patient's mood and decreasing his perceptions of pain. Episodes of acute pain can sometimes be controlled by listening to loud, lively rock-type music, and snapping your fingers to the rhythm.

• **Sometimes our reaction to music is more powerful than we expect.** Hearing a song that makes our heart stop—something that brings back our teenage years or an unrequited love, for instance—is testimony to the potency of music. We can use music as a wonderful therapy, but we must respect it and handle it with care. There are some places in our past we prefer not to return.

• **Friends and loved ones can help by sharing music—tapes, CDs, even playing music for us, live. But they need to deter-**

mine what type of music will be most enjoyable for the patient and family. Your favorite is classical, hers is country. You like a good Broadway tune, he finds release with hardcore rock 'n' roll. And since caregivers and patients both benefit from music therapy, there are bound to be conflicts. **Earplugs and headphones are an inexpensive solution. Make certain the *patient* has control over musical choices, as well as volume.** Otherwise, music can be a painful nuisance to someone who is very ill.

My sister is staying with me now, and I don't want to have to go to a nursing home. I want her to be happy so she'll stay. But she has always loved gospel music. She brought all her tapes and she plays them all day long. The stereo is in the living room where we've moved my bed. I don't want to complain—her music is the only thing she has. I think she just figures I enjoy it, too. I try not to be obvious about it, but I just have to turn my head to the wall and crush the pillow against my ear. It isn't so bad. I can ignore it, most times. It's better than having to leave my house, that's for sure.

- **To determine a person's reactions to music, it helps to ask a few getting-to-know-you questions,** such as, "What kind of music did you hear when you were growing up?" and "What kind of music do you most like to listen to now?" **After listening to music together, we can ask and share still more.** For instance, "What did this music remind you of?" Or, "How does that song make you feel?" Or, "Do those lyrics have any particular meaning?" And so on.

ART

- **By *art* I do not mean only paintings and sculpture. I mean any object created and enjoyed for its presence as well as its function.** Pastries. Furniture. Photographs. Quilts. Jewelry. Flower gardens. And yes, paintings and sculptures. Art is created from various tangible materials; what we choose to see or create are metaphors that help us find the meanings and values in our own lives.

• **A healthy therapy is to put a little art into everything.** Place special, beautiful objects near the patient's resting area. Put a spray of dried flowers beside the sink in the bathroom. Keep important medications in a special antique box or on a lovely silver tray, instead of just cluttered together on a shelf. Make a special effort to use pretty dishes and place settings for meals. Pay attention to the aesthetics in the environment.

• **Find opportunities to be creative with an ill loved one and the family of caregivers.** Here are just a few ideas for projects to create, along with patients and their loved ones:

songwriting	*playwriting*	*photo albums*	*collages*
bookbinding	*sweaters*	*embroidering*	*sewing*
leather tooling	*watercolors*	*tapestries*	*weaving*
woodworking	*pottery*	*children's books*	*cookies*
quilts	*fishing flies*	*ceramics*	*afghans*
doll clothes	*toys*	*doll furniture*	*flower boxes*
candles	*baskets*	*jewelry*	*jams/jellies*
family trees	*cake decorating*	*finger paintings*	*crocheting*
herb gardens	*beading*	*singing*	*reading poetry*
models	*choreography*	*bread*	

• **Many patients and loved ones may put up barriers to these ideas. Ironically, they might be even more likely to resist if they were particularly artistic before the illness.** They become discouraged because they feel they can't do the same things they once did. All this is understandable. Making things is physical work, and it takes energy and concentration. Remind them that it also relieves stress and—when appropriate—tactfully suggest that artwork can become a beautiful legacy.

• **Some activities may need to be modified.** Perhaps the fine furniture making of your husband is no longer feasible, but he build a beautiful jewelry box for his granddaughter. If fine motor skills are no longer trustworthy, find an activity that requires less detail work and patience. For example, your sister's tiny doilies become a crocheted afghan. Or her lace making itself turns into a legacy, as she teaches *you* how to make doilies. **When in doubt, try it!** We may not immediately think of baking sugar cookies in bed, but it's been done (and it can be lots of fun).

* **Friends and loved ones help when they offer ideas or bring gifts of supplies for the various artists in the patient's family.** Paints, papers, yarn, clay, cooking ingredients, for example. But unsolicited ideas for the family's activities are just that—unsolicited! Make suggestions and offers, but *don't push*.

* **Also remember that many supplies are already available, right at home.** The kitchen is a wealth of resources. If your friend has the reputation of world-class cook, come over and make spaghetti with her. And the house is probably already full of photographs just waiting to be put into beautiful albums, if only a thoughtful friend brought by the books and got the family started. Or how about a collage or nature mobile? The materials are as close as the backyard.

My brother died of AIDS in 1989. We'd always gone camping and hiking when we were kids, and a few months before he died he wanted to go back to the north shore of Lake Superior. We rented a cabin for a few days, and one morning he had enough energy to go on a little hike down on the rocks below our cabin. We collected these sticks that had been smoothed by the waves—sun bleached and plain. We found this little rock, and Marty also found a gull feather. Just silly little treasures, nothing very special.

It started to rain so we went back to the cabin, lit a fire, and tried to think of something to do. Marty found some fishing twine in a drawer and said, "Hey, let's make a mobile out of the stuff from our hike!" He was an engineer. He really got into making sure it was perfectly balanced. I will never forget that afternoon. We laughed so hard and had so much fun.

When we got home, he hung the mobile in his living room. Later, when we moved his bed out there, he used to stare at it all the time. Just a few days before he died, he told me, "Annie, our artwork from up north has been perfect for me. It has reminded me—it all boils down to finding balance. You take it after I'm gone. It will remind you, too."

Our mobile hangs over my desk at home. I look at it and think about Marty and what he taught me nearly every single day. If you saw it, you might even laugh: just four little sticks, a common feather, a not-so-special rock. But for me, it's priceless. If my house ever burned down, it's the one thing I'd grab first.

DEEP BREATHING

- **One of the easiest therapies of all is breath control.** We've heard it since we were little kids: "Take ten deep breaths first, to calm down."

- **Before investing much time in breathing exercises, first make sure you're breathing *correctly*, from the diaphragm.** Take a deep breath and look at yourself in profile. If your stomach sucks in and your chest expands, you are breathing incorrectly. **Instead, breathe so that when you inhale, your stomach sticks out instead of in, and your chest is completely collapsed at first.** Fill the bottom half of your lungs first, and only then expand your chest to fill the top half. After this correct breath, your lungs will be filled to their entire capacity.

- **The idea of diaphragm breathing isn't easy to grasp.** Ask a friend who has taken **voice lessons,** or do what some people do: lie on the floor with a **five-pound bag of flour on your stomach,** breathing to make the bag rise on each inhale.

- **Once you're able to fill your lungs to capacity at will, you can begin doing so in a regular, rhythmic fashion whenever you want.** It's one of the fastest, easiest ways to help yourself feel calmer and more refreshed.

MEDITATION

- **Meditation generally involves just a few necessary ingredients—twenty minutes of private, uninterrupted time, and a straight-backed chair.** A cushioned wheelchair works well for patients, or for bedridden loved ones, raise the bed to the most comfortable upright position.

  - **Sit comfortably but upright** in your chair or bed with your feet placed flat on the floor or footrests, or with your back against the headboard and your legs extended. Lightly rest your hands on your lap, palms up. Close your eyes gently and begin to breathe slowly and deeply. With each exhale, imagine breathing out all the stress and tension in your body. With each breath, imagine a new part of your body becoming relaxed. Start with your head, then your neck, shoulders, down each arm, each hand, torso, hips, thighs, calves, and finally feet, one new body area relaxing with each breath. Take a few minutes to do this.

  - **When your body feels relaxed, shift your attention to a focal point.** This may be visual—a candle, a treasured object. It may be audible—a word you say in your head, in rhythm with each exhaled breath. Try to choose a word that has special meaning, and one with an *s* sound in it, because you will hear hissing when you say these words in your head, which will heighten the sensation of "breathing out" your stress. One good choice is the word *peace.* Another good choice is *balance.* And another still is *release.* Choose whatever works best for you.

  - **Just breathe in and out slowly, concentrating on the rhythm and on your focal point. When other thoughts enter your mind, just observe them and let them go. After several**

minutes, you won't need to struggle with your brain so much. The word or focal point is taking a deeper meaning. You actually feel peace, or balance. You can actually imagine yourself the light of the candle. You feel deeply relaxed and calm—completely in the moment. Enjoy this experience for several more minutes. When you feel quite refreshed, take a deep breath, stretching your whole body as you take in that air. Fully exhale that breath. Take one more deep breath as you slowly open your eyes, rejoining the world around you.

IMAGERY

- **Imagery is useful for taking us to beautiful places when our bodies can't make the trip. A common form of stress relief is to imagine a postcard**—imposing mountains, seashore with mesmerizing waves, forest meadow, whatever your personal preference. Keep that picture in your mind for several minutes; spend this time adding and noticing the details. You'll feel refreshed after making this journey. Incidentally, this form of escape is being used in hospice for pain management, with encouraging success for many patients. It can be **enhanced by listening to background sound** CDs and cassettes—ocean waves, rainstorms, and so forth.

- **Guided imagery exercises are still another form of therapy. We transport ourselves mentally to a specific place, and typically ask questions and seek answers in our imaginations. The answers often appear** to us in these exercises, demonstrating our capacity for self-healing and awareness. Each of us has our own private doctor (or prophet) within.

- **When performing a ten- to fifteen-minute guided imagery exercise, first lie down in a comfortable position.** Your eyes should be closed and it helps to darken the room. A friend or loved one can enhance this exercise for you by reading the script of a guided imagery story, such as the example below. Or you can tape it yourself, then play back your tape anytime you want to do the exercise. (Be sure to read slowly!) Or, if you don't want to ask for help from a friend and you're not excited about hearing your own voice on tape, these imagery exercises will work just fine if you imagine the sequences yourself. Just be careful not to rush yourself. Here is an example; also try writing your own.

- **The Doors**   You are walking down a path through the forest. Notice the scenery, the animals, plants. Smell the fragrances. What temperature is it? What are you wearing? Experience the weather. Suddenly you come upon a door. You try to open it; you struggle. What does the door look like? What is it made of? You struggle and struggle, and suddenly the door opens. Someone is waiting for you. Who is it? What does this person want? Have a conversation with this person. (Wait several minutes.) You decide to leave this place. You continue down the forest path; you are back in nature again. Notice your surroundings. Are they any different than they were before you opened that door? As you continue walking, you see another door. You walk up to it, you begin to open it, you think you'll have to struggle, but it opens quite easily. You walk into the room. What does this room look like? What colors do you notice? Do you hear anything? Yes, you hear footsteps. Someone is coming down a hallway. You turn and find yourself facing this person. Who is it? What do you see? Have a conversation with this person. (Wait several minutes.) You leave this room and walk back down the forest path. You're thinking about these two people you met and what you talked about. You feel peaceful, refreshed after your walk. You notice the path is leading here, to your home. You gently walk into the house, come into this room, and lie down to rest and think about this walk some more. (Wait several minutes.) When you feel rested, slowly open your eyes.

- **It's also helpful for many families to be aware that guided imagery can be effective in honest-to-goodness *physical* pain management.** Many hospice nurses are using guided imagery therapies in a clinical, professional setting with their incurable clients. The nurses build metaphors for patients such as putting out painful fires with ice, or squeezing out an especially troublesome condition, or imagining warm waves rolling over various parts of the body.

VENTING

- It's healthy to get things off our chest, but lots of times, the people or situations that have injured us are in our very environment, and it doesn't help matters to get vocal about everything. Happy households **pick their battles.** It helps when each family member has outlets—more than one if possible—for **private venting.** This way, the loved ones can expel their hurts and angers alone and safely, without polluting the household atmosphere. Try these methods for healthy venting (some need modifying for physically weak patients or loved ones):

  - Lie facedown on your bed with your face in a pillow. Yell, scream, and cry. Pound your fists on the mattress and kick your feet. Do this until you are completely tired.

  - Grab a pad of paper, or sheets of newspaper. Think about who and what has upset you. Write on the page the person's name or a feeling you have or something that was said. Write whatever word or phrase comes to mind. Say that phrase out loud, then crumple the paper, or rip it up, stomp on it, even throw it across the room. Then take a fresh piece of paper, write down the next phrase, repeat the process. Keep writing and destroying until you can't think of any more phrases to write, say, and mutilate.

  - Use both hands to hold a tennis racket over your head; smash it down in front of you on top of the mattress lots of times in a row, until you are tired.

  - Roll up an old magazine or newspaper and bang it against the door frame as you shout out the things you feel upset about. (Note: If you do this when you are alone in the house, you can even shout out a family member's name. That can be a *very* therapeutic release!)

- Find a screaming room: a parked closed-up car in a private place, a closet with a pillow over your face, under a railroad bridge when the train goes by.

- Sing at the top of your lungs in the car.

- Buy some bongo drums. Bang on the piano.

- Twist a towel. Have a pull fight with your dog (or a friend).

- Go for a long, hard, fast walk. With each step, say the name of the person who has upset you and shout out loud what you wish you could say, in time to your marching steps.

- Use the famous empty-chair technique: Imagine the person who wronged you sits in the chair across from you. Tell this person just what you think.

- Go to a football, hockey, or basketball game and shout your lungs out.

- Dig a hole in the backyard or in the woods. Make it deep. Really exert yourself as you dig, saying the person's name or what upset you with every strike of the shovel. When you are exhausted, stop digging and rest for a moment. Then speak your remaining angers and frustrations into the empty hole. Take as long as you need. Then fill the hole back up with dirt. Bury those angers, and finish by stomping on them.

- Watch a whole bunch of action-thriller movies in a row and scream during all the scary parts. (Probably most effective when performed in privacy.)

- Do some strenuous physical exercise, like playing tennis or racquetball or running sprints.

- Clean out the basement, garage, or attic—a cleansing metaphor to think about while getting exercise and completing a major task.

HUMOR

- **We've heard it, and it's true; our bodies really *do* release endor-phins—feel-good chemicals—whenever we laugh and smile. Even if nothing funny has happened, we can make ourselves feel better just by laughing out loud. So laugh, just for the sheer exercise of it.** Make yourself guffaw and belly-jiggle, even if it's a forced-sounding har-har-har at first. Get your whole body into it, slapping your knees and shaking your head. Chortle and heh-heh-heh in lots of different voices. Laugh as you imagine a lion would, a hyena, a monkey. Just *make yourself* do the physi-cal act even without any reason. You'll feel better and maybe start smiling for real. By the way, you might want to do the above in pri-vate, unless you're ready to give the rest of your family a *real* laugh!

- Rent a bunch of Jerry Lewis movies or old grade-B horror movies; watch *Nick at Nite* on cable television. Pull out your old records. Watch reruns of *Saturday Night Live*. Read the newspaper comics. Laugh, *every* day.

- **Express yourself with humor, whenever possible. Make the commitment to find at least one thing funny every single day.** Really *look* for that something. When you find it, tell someone else about it.

DOING FOR OTHERS

- **The idea of random acts of kindness has taken hold in our country,** at least in theory. With these acts, we reach out to total strangers, passing out unexpected gifts and generosities, and we hope our efforts multiply. These fun and easy therapies are the perfect way to increase warm feelings in ourselves, particularly if much of our life has been involved with doctors and illness. Here are some ideas I've recently heard:

  - Pay the toll for your own car, and *also* for the car after you

  - Give a pack of Life Savers to the bus driver

- Go to a shopping mall and hand out flowers, each with a tag saying "Feel glad today—and pass this flower on to someone else." Then sit back and watch, as the flowers change hands and joy spreads.

- **Make it your family's goal to put the random-acts theory into practice. What a happy way for family members to relieve stress.** Each week, plan, perform, and share the results of at least one random act of kindness. This activity can be shared by family members of all ages and all conditions. *Everyone* can play some part.

- **Choose a family activity that "does for others" in even *bigger* ways.** Make a commitment to work once a month at a shelter. Or make a Sunday afternoon ritual of taking a family walk while collecting litter. Volunteer at your hospital. Take your pets to the nursing home. Offer to speak in your area schools to educate kids about the illness.

- **It's trite but true: The quickest way for us to help ourselves is to help somebody else.** You readers already know this; your eyes wouldn't be resting on this page in the first place if you weren't committed to helping a family you love.

I was walking with a friend down a city street when suddenly I heard "plink." I looked on the sidewalk behind us and saw a dime.

"Diane," I said, "you dropped some money." Her eyes twinkled, and she said, "I know," and kept on walking.

"Don't you want to pick it up?" I asked.

"No, I did it on purpose." I raised my eyebrows, so she explained. "Didn't you love to find money when you were little? I had twelve kids in my family, and if I ever found a nickel or a dime in the street, I was happy for days. I thought I was the richest kid in the world when that happened. So that's why I drop change when I walk, so some kid will find it and feel lucky."

"What if some scuzzy old bum picks it up instead?" I challenged.

"That's okay. He needs to feel lucky, too, I guess. I don't really care who picks it up. I just like imagining how happy and surprised they feel when they find it."

And a few more times that afternoon, I heard "plink." We'd walk a few more blocks, then "plink." It was the sweetest little sound.

NOTES

18

CARING FOR
FAMILY CAREGIVER

- **The average patient requires a family caregiver to provide seventy hours per week of care** (this figure includes the hours spent at home "because someone has to be here all the time"). These hours, nearly the equivalent of two full-time jobs, are often in addition to a "real" full-time job. And sadly, research on caregiving shows that when **a competent caregiver is already in place, other family members don't do as much as they could to help.** Unfortunately, friends don't fill in the gaps, either.

- **A major complaint among caregivers is fatigue, compounded by isolation.** We go to work, then come home to work some more. We wake up the next day to do it all over again. No vacation, 365 days a year, and many caregivers spend more than a *decade* in this role. That's why caregiver burnout is prevalent.

- **Providing care for a seriously ill loved one is an extremely demanding responsibility; we must cope *physically, mentally, and spiritually.*** Caregiver stress appears, and frequently, in these ways:

  PHYSICAL: headache; muscle ache; sleeping and eating problems; fatigue; weight loss or gain; heaviness in the chest; worsening chronic conditions; diarrhea; upset stomach

  MENTAL: forgetfulness; poor concentration and attention; feelings of guilt or anger; difficulty making decisions; impatience; crying spells; sensitivity to criticism; blaming; depression; anxiety

  SPIRITUAL: alienation; loss of hope, purpose, or meaning; feeling useless; pessimism about the past, present, and future; obsession about death; thinking more than usual about one's own death; feelings of futility

- **The physical demands of caregiving require strength and stamina**—the need to complete countless additional household tasks, physically tending to and moving the patient, operating with interrupted sleep, and with less time to tend to our own physical needs. Obviously, it helps if as caregivers we can guard our own physical health as much as possible by adopting regular exercise, nutritious meals and snacks, moderate to no chemical consumption, and other healthy lifestyle habits.

- **Mentally, caregivers cope with a wide array of confusing thoughts and feelings, some private, others public. If you or someone you love has feelings like these, welcome to normalcy:**

  "I'm overwhelmed. I can't seem to do anything right."

  "I'm angry. I get irritated over nothing."

  "I've distanced myself from everyone."

  "I just wish this would be over."

  "I feel like a fake. I don't know if I even love him anymore."

  "I feel jealous because he gets all the attention."

  "I guess I probably deserved this."

  "I wish people could see what this has done to my life."

  "I'm too boring to see anyone. My life is all drudgery."

  "I can't do this anymore. I don't care about anything."

  "I keep forgetting the littlest things. I just can't concentrate."

- **Caregiving in a spiritual sense is complicated and loaded with contradictions.** On the one hand, we may view this experience as a "trial" or "test," perhaps even a punishment. On the other, we view it as an opportunity to provide service, to contribute, to live

out the Golden Rule on a daily basis. Beneath all these contradictions lies a fundamental question, What does this illness mean
in the Big Scheme of things? If my loved one can be daunted by
disease this way, what's in store for me?

- **Friends need to take special care when they hear a caregiver
express negativity. Our first instinct is to calm and comfort,
which we try to do by "taking away" the hurt or doubts—but
this can be a big mistake!** For instance, we tell our sister, "How
could you possibly think you *deserve* this! You've been a saint, your
whole life!" This loving remark actually closes off the conversation
and robs our sister of a valuable opportunity to vent her scary questions and negative feelings. A much more helpful response would
be, "You say you probably deserved this? That sounds interesting . . . tell me how!" **Later, we can offer her our reassurances,
but only *after* she's had a chance to fully express her fears and
angers.**

- **When we experience burnout, a common feeling is, "What's
wrong with me!?"** We spend far too much time allowing our
friends and loved ones to think something's wrong with us. We
spend too much time trying to fix ourselves. **A more helpful
question is, What's wrong with this *situation,* and how can
it be changed** to reduce these very normal, though stressful,
reactions?

- **What's wrong with the situation is actually fairly obvious; the
caregiver is overworked. Plain and simple, she needs *help and
respite.*** This is where loving friends and family prove invaluable.

- **Within our family, seeking help can be difficult.** We don't
want to burden family members with the physical elements of
caregiving; we don't want them to feel obligated to us. Yet research
in caregiving shows that **many physical care and hygiene tasks
are better performed at least part of the time by someone *outside the family* who can be *objective.*** This affords more dignity
and privacy to the patient, and provides tremendous relief for the

family caregiver. After all, it isn't easy to give your own father a bath, much less an enema.

- **Family and friends can perhaps pool together funds to hire a home health aide** to visit three times per week, thirty to sixty minutes per visit, to perform such routine physical care tasks as baths, manicures, and hairwashes. Check the Yellow Pages under Home Care.

- **Another worthwhile investment is hiring a private clinical social worker, for just an hour or two of consulting.** This may cost $100 to $200 and might not be covered by insurance, but this professional can save the family scads of time and money by helping us locate specific disease-related support groups in our region, advising us about volunteer agencies that provide free respite, obtaining home-care equipment, advising us about financial assistance programs, helping with guardianship concerns, and providing all-around guidance on countless other aspects of our situation. Look in the Yellow Pages under Social Workers for names and numbers, or call the National Association of Social Workers to ask for members in your area (see Helpful Organizations, p. 211).

- **When looking for other objective outsiders,** contact your **local hospital,** the patient's **medical team,** and any **regional or national organization** that supports families living with a specific disease. Use **hotlines,** call the local **library,** visit a **local bookstore.** Contact both the local **Chamber of Commerce** and local **city or county government center** to inquire about inexpensive private and nonprofit services that might be available. It also helps to know that many **churches have a visiting nurse or a pool of volunteers who make home visits.** Don't worry, they are typically trained *not* to espouse their beliefs during a visit. For families living with end-stage illness, contact **hospice programs** in your county. Many people don't realize they are eligible for no-cost home-care and social services.

- **Close friends help tremendously when they offer to do this information seeking *for* the family.** Anyone who has tried to track down even *one* social service agency knows the process can take an entire morning. A patient and loved ones are far too busy, distracted, and perhaps more easily frustrated. A close friend can be more tolerant of the need to play phone tag; we are also likely to be more objective when hearing what these resources might—and might not—be able to offer this family we love.

- **Perhaps the biggest gift our friends provide is by offering regular, tangible respite.** It really is true that friends want to know *specifically* how to help. We feel just as hollow and silly saying, "Can I do anything?" as the patient and family members do when answering, "Oh no, we're just fine, really."

- **The next time a friend asks, "Is there anything I can do?" we need to speak up and say, "Yes—if you're *really* willing, you could sign up for a task on the family roster!"**

- **On the following page is a sample roster of all the household and caretaking jobs a family could easily farm out to others.** Caregivers and the patients they love can custom-tailor this roster to include their own special needs.

- **And as with information seeking, this roster is often more useful when the idea is suggested and ultimately managed by a close friend, since *non*family members are generally less shy about recruiting volunteers.** Take the initiative, best friend! Your caregiving loved one would probably never ask you to do this, but the family's life can greatly improve if you do.

PUT YOUR NAME AND PHONE # IN THE BLANK WHERE YOU COULD OFFER REGULAR HELP

- 2 loads laundry per week: Mon _____ Thurs _____
  (beds stripped, laundry picked up, done off-site, delivered 2–3
    days later)

- 1 dinner prepared off-site, delivered weekly, pick up pans
    following week:
    Mon _____ Wed _____ Fri _____ Sun _____

- 1–2 hours dust/vacuum common living areas weekly: _____

- 1–2 hours dust/vacuum sleeping areas weekly: _____

- 1 hour cleaning patient area weekly: _____

- 1 hour bathroom cleaning weekly: Upstairs _____
                                     Downstairs _____

- 1–2 hours kitchen cleaning, floors scrubbed weekly: _____

- 4-hour respite care weekly: Mon _____ Wed _____
                                Fri _____ Sat _____

- Patient bathing and hygiene: Mon _____ Tues _____
                                 Wed _____ Thurs _____ Sat _____

- 1 overnight monthly: _____

- 1 hour grocery shopping weekly: Tue _____ Fri _____

- 1 hour errands weekly: _____

- 1 hour yard work weekly: _____

- 1 hour car maintenance (gas, wash, fluid/tire check) weekly: _____

- 1 hour weekly banking/bill paying: _____

- Will drive to appts on call: _____

- Other ways I could help: _____

- **It really isn't difficult to find helpers when we keep the tasks basic, regular, and break them down so that each requires only one to two hours every week or so.** We need to discourage friends from signing on for more, otherwise they won't be able to perform over the long haul. And remember, even one hour a week is a much more generous commitment than most people will ever make to this family.

- **And of course, friends ought to sign up only for jobs they care to handle.** For example, any responsible adult can be trained to give the patient a bath, but friends only add stress to the family by agreeing to help with this highly personal task if they are squeamish about it in any way.

- **Once people sign on, it is essential to stick to the schedule as closely as possible;** the family is already coping with a host of interruptions, and we help most when we don't bother them with scheduling problems or changes. (This is another good reason to have a nonfamily member handle the roster.) Helpers need to fulfill their responsibility or find a replacement—**friends call the roster manager with changes or conflicts, *not* the family.**

- **It helps when friends do as much as they can off-site, whenever possible.** Meals, laundry, and bill paying can be accomplished at *our* houses, not the family's. We can also **combine jobs;** a person providing four hours of respite care can likely accomplish some major housework during that very same visit. People helping the family in their home are also wise to appreciate that it's less stressful on the family members when they **come primarily to do their job and then depart.** An additional five- to ten-minute visit may be welcomed, but be sensitive: socializing even this briefly can quickly sap the family's energy. And energy is something the patients and caregivers alike are trying hard to conserve.

- **Sometimes a patient initially balks about having outsiders help.** She may say to the primary caregiver, "I don't *want* anybody else around, *especially* not for a whole morning! Only *you* can do this for me!" **Likewise, caregivers often allow themselves to feel indispensable:** "I am the only one who makes him really comfortable—besides, I don't *want* anyone else cleaning our dirty bathrooms!" These are very common hurdles, and ones that are wisest to overcome, for the well-being and sanity of the entire family. **A trusted person can firmly explain to the resistant patient or caregiver,** "We are not offering this help just for *you*, but for the entire family. There are so many things we *can't* do for you—please allow us to do what we *can*, so you can continue to deal with this situation as well as you are."

- **Even cranky or difficult patients and caregivers will soon grow accustomed to having other people around, and even *like* it,** especially if it's the same people doing the same tasks, on a weekly schedule. The regular comings and goings help mark the calendar; after just a few weeks the individual family members even look forward to these visits. They provide the chance to be with someone other than the "same old" people. And any home-care worker will tell you that patients and their loved ones relish the opportunity to have a new audience and a fresh perspective.

- One of the most important things we can do for this family—far more important than dusting or snow shoveling—is to **offer them respite.** In short, it helps to get the patient and individual family members away from each other (and, indirectly, from the situation) on a frequent and regular basis. Take the patient on outings—alone. Take each kid overnight—separately. Stay at the patient's home every Monday morning, between nine and one. **Truly generous friends stay overnight with the patient, or for a weekend.** When a few of us pool these evenings—each of us staying only forty-eight hours or so—we enable a caregiver to do what she wants or go where she wants for at least a week: a definite burnout buster!

- **At first, friends who want to provide respite care might be hesitant because of physical care concerns and worries about potential emergencies.** "I don't know how to work a wheelchair." "I feel embarrassed about helping another person in the bathroom."

"What if she gets sicker and I'm the only one responsible?" And the *truly* scary, "What if he *dies* while I'm here?" We are helped by remembering that for any seriously ill patient, medical expertise is instantly available, twenty-four hours a day.

- **Taking care of a very sick person is mostly common sense.** After all, the family members were novices once, too, and look how well *they* are doing. Reading certain sections in **this book's appendix** will help. In just a few short pages, respite volunteers can become acquainted with the basics of physical care. The **first visit is always the most awkward,** but caring for a seriously ill person is just like caring for anything else really—a new baby, a wounded bird, a stray kitten. We call on others for expertise when we need to, but we do best when we **follow our instincts.** And with incurable people—versus babies, birds, and kittens—we have the added advantage that **the patient can talk to us** about what she needs. In a short time, confidence about physical caregiving won't be an issue.

- **Giving time each week, and consistently, is a big commitment. Sometimes we don't feel appreciated; we begin to wonder if we're even making a difference. But stop to consider this behind-the-scenes scenario:** Last night, the caregiver was up at three, stripping sheets because of an accident. And the patient felt sad about it—even a little guilty—though he tried hard not to. Still, they both felt better than they might have, because they knew a good friend was coming by in the morning. And now, that loving friend is handling the laundry and playing cards with the patient, while the caregiver is out for a long walk with her best friend.

- **Helpful loved ones can give just one or two hours per week—and collectively make all the difference in the world.**

NOTES

19

THE VISIT:
GIFTS AND GOOD TIDINGS

- **Friends and loved ones provide vital companionship** to a family living with incurable illness. This voyage shows the true depths of our friendships. Many so-called friends no longer stop by, much less phone, while some friends who *weren't* so close now become true stalwarts. It's surprising sometimes.

Two close friends of mine are twin sisters—Lucy and Barbara. Lucy has been battling cancer, pretty seriously, for the past few months. The two have always been inseparable. Neither married, they share a house, they share everything, even a close circle of friends. Of course most friends are closer to one twin than the other. There's one friend, Millie, who is a friend of Lucy's from work. Barbara never really seemed to like Millie that much. She cared about her because Lucy does but she's always been pretty sarcastic about her. She's seemed to tolerate Millie more than like her.

The last time I talked to Barbara, she said, "I can't believe how wonderful Millie has been. She comes over after work a few evenings a week and helps me take care of Lucy. Most of my friends seem to have dropped off the face of the earth. But not Millie. We talk and laugh. She's coming over tonight. She's going to make her great lasagna. And she's funny, too. I don't know why I didn't see it before."

- **The best gifts we can bring to a family living with illness is *ourselves.*** A companion, a chum for the patient—someone to take him for a country drive, or to a favorite bookstore, or just to sit quietly by his bed. This gift does double duty; it also provides time away for the caregiver. Just call the family to say, "I'll be over to play cards with Jim at about eleven. I can stay until four, so maybe you could make plans to get your hair cut and see that movie."

- **Respite visits are quite different than social visits.** When providing respite, we should stay as long as we're able—**at least three and preferably four hours.** A caregiving loved one can barely *get* anywhere, much less do much for herself, when we only stay an hour or two.

- **When making a respite visit, helpful friends make it clear that we are *not* there to be entertained.** Instead we're there to provide the comfort of a responsible presence. Therefore, let the family members know directly that we **always bring something to do on a respite visit** (a good book, letters to write, work not completed in the office) for those times the patient or family members prefer to be left alone. **Remember—keeping out of the way is sometimes the very best thing a good friend can do.**

- **Things to do on a respite visit:** write letters for the patient, read to the patient, give a massage, tidy the bathroom/kitchen, mow the lawn, give the patient a manicure, apply makeup, give the patient a bath, give the dog a bath, dust and vacuum, wash a window, weed the garden, walk the dog, do the grocery shopping, pick up prescriptions, run errands, provide transport to appointments, "chum" with the patient (play cards, share lunch, talk, go on country drives, look at old photographs, share hobbies). **Things to bring on a respite visit:** book, magazine, stationery and pen, surgical gloves (for certain types of physical care), lotion for hand massages, handiwork, a snack, a journal, playing cards, tissues, a transfer belt, emergency info, The ABCs of Physical Care (p. 193).

- Respite visits offer tangible support; social visits offer symbolic and emotional support. **Friends who drop by just to chat need to be careful not to overstay their welcome**—twenty minutes is usually more than ample. In the last stages of illness, even five minutes can exhaust the patient.

- **It isn't necessary to cheer someone up on any social visit, nor should we feel we must bring only good news.** We don't need to entertain, hide our own problems, or otherwise placate. It's best when we talk just as normally and naturally as before.

- **When visiting a family even socially, the most helpful friends also make it a point to find something *constructive* to contribute.** If we see a sink full of dishes, we do them. If the bushes need a trim, we go out in the garage to find the pruning shears. Or offer to make lunch, and when we look in the fridge and find no milk, we make up a shopping list and run errands. These are the gifts that count.

- **In addition to bringing an open ear and a willing-to-work smile, helpful friends and loved ones often want to bring real gifts. And gift-giving *anytime* can be a sticky issue, but especially when faced with incurable illness.** We ponder and deliberate. We want to show our affection, but we are scared we might choose something that will be totally useless or, even worse, a "slap in the face" to the patient or family members.

- **The best gifts come from the heart.** Yes, we may make mistakes in our choices sometimes, but loved ones will always overlook any effrontery in the face of the larger gesture we are making. We shouldn't worry so much; perhaps this chapter can provide some guidance. After we've sent the plants and flowers, we can try these other ideas, too.

- **Food gifts are very appropriate for caregivers, especially if they constitute an entree**—a spiral-cut ham, for example, or a heavy soup or special quiche or salad. And it helps to be more original than the typical hamburger or tuna casserole.

- **Food gifts are *less* appropriate for patients, especially in the final stages of illness.** Yes, some patients do develop cravings for a particular fruit or brand of soup, but eating needs generally become minimal. It helps to find out the cravings and periodically supply them, bearing in mind that these tastes can change overnight, and unsolicited treats sometimes bring only pressure and sadness as the patient loses her taste for certain foods.

I was visiting one of the patients in our hospice program when a doctor friend came to call. She's very compassionate, but also very young. I don't think she's had much experience with dying yet. She had just been on a wonderful trip to England, and she brought back a present for Valerie—a huge box of expensive chocolates. She said, "Now this is special, luxury stuff, and you deserve only the very best—so promise me you'll eat a piece!"

After she left, Valerie shrugged her shoulders and silently handed the box to her husband. No one said anything, but we were all probably thinking the same thing; just 45 minutes earlier we'd all shared the sorrow of Valerie eating only a tiny spoonful of oatmeal before pushing the bowl away. She'd cried and said, "Now I really know I'm getting to the end. Even this glop I can't eat anymore!"

• **Gifts of clothing can be a wonderful gesture, especially clothing that is finely made, functional, and *beautiful.*** Contrary to what many people think, seriously ill people do *not* spend most of their time in pajamas. Instead, they typically get up every day, bathe, and wear daytime outfits that are comfortable for lots of rest time, but also suitable for visitors and outings. **But clothing, especially slacks, can be a real problem and source of anxiety for patients,** because people often lose weight very rapidly in the last stages of illness and their old wardrobe seems to fall off their body. Clothes that fit just a few weeks earlier no longer feel comfortable or attractive.

• **Choose pull-on slacks and tops in decreasing sizes as the illness progresses.** Avoid zippers, buttons, or anything that would poke. Choose cotton materials that breathe and that are also easy to wash and dry. **By the same token, don't choose clothes that are so functional as to be ugly.** Go beyond sweatsuits. Choose a vibrant, favorite color of the patient's, a fashionable angular cut. Hand paint, cross-stitch, or appliqué a pretty T-neck. When deciding, ask yourself this question: Would I feel attractive in this outfit when running errands as well as comfortable in it, when curled up for a nap?

- **Gifts of music are another source of pleasure for both patient and caregivers. A portable CD player or cassette player might be greatly appreciated, with a selection of the family's favorite music.** Something small and uncomplicated is more helpful than a model with all the whistles and bells. It needs to fit on a shelf or table, within easy reach of the patient. And since friends and other volunteers will be offering respite, we don't want to choose something that needs an owner's manual to operate.

- **Books on tape are another idea and may be even preferable to the real thing.** As I've said earlier, few seriously ill people have the energy to actually hold up a book and read it, and primary caregivers are far too busy. But many enjoyable hours can be spent *listening* together; the words can float through the rooms as the caregiver gives a bath, changes the linens, or completes other household and caregiving tasks.

- **Helpful friends take care in selecting reading material. It's probably wiser to err in favor of too light than too heavy.** Some well-meaning people make the mistake of almost romanticizing serious illness; they imagine ill people as finally having the opportunity to do those cerebral things we often don't make time for when we are more physically active. They imagine people reading the classics, or the great philosophers, or doing lots of journal writing. In reality, these priorities are rarely important. **When life is in its final stages, concentration on the material world becomes difficult if not downright uninteresting.** The patient is more likely turning *inward* now, with extremely powerful *private* concerns, and not as much interest in the external world and surroundings.

- **It's also easy to make the mistake of soapboxing through the gifts we choose for others. We are sometimes too anxious to share the spiritual or physical approaches that have been meaningful in our own lives.** Incurably ill people and their loved ones are frequently inundated with lots of must-read material. "This book was *so* wonderful," friends say. "You just *have* to read it; I know it will help you as much as it helped me." Or, "You *have* to make this recipe—I've brought all the ingredients. People in Sweden have found it slows the progress of cancer."

I remember one person from work giving me a whole folder full of health-food diet stuff. Broccoli juice and everything. I took one look at it and laughed right in her face—I couldn't help it, it struck me so funny. I said, "Yvonne, I really appreciate your gesture, but you have to know something. My husband has never eaten a vegetable in his life he didn't complain about. He's always said the most efficient method of eating is out of a white paper bag. And now that he's gotten this prognosis, he's more determined than ever to eat anything he wants. As he says, what difference does it make now?"

- **We need to consider the philosophical dimension of our gifts. Are we preaching in any way?** Do our choices presuppose that *our* approach is better or more preferable than the family's? We need to avoid imposing our values on this family anytime, but especially when giving them gifts.

- **A camcorder is a good idea for many families.** It can provide many moments of fun and a wonderful legacy, not just of the patient but also of this time. Perhaps you know of a camera the family could borrow, or where you might rent one for a few weeks. And if you're a friend of the family and good with a camera, you could come over with tapes and offer to do the filming.

- **Take portraits of the family.** Yes, even at this time. In fact many experts advise us to take photos *especially* at this time; they provide a beautiful legacy and help us appreciate later what we accomplished on this journey. Provide a pretty album for housing them.

- **Offer to help catalog and preserve a collection** the family treasures such as a library of books or old record albums, for example.

- **An overnight stay in a luxury hotel** is a fabulous gift for a weary caregiver. Pool resources and include respite care for the patient. Have one friend order a fruit basket for the room, still another can provide the certificate for a massage in the hotel's salon. **You can also pool resources to send the entire family on vacation.** This does not have to be as expensive as it sounds. Seven days in a cabin by a lake can be accomplished for a few hundred dollars. That's just thirty dollars apiece, spread among a dozen or so loved ones and friends. Or, you can send the whole family overnight to a fun hotel with an indoor pool and sauna.

- **A weekly trip to the library is a nice present—and it's free!** Choose videos, documentaries, music, and books on tape for the entire family, and each week *be responsible for returning them.* Make a gift of continuous, completely hassle-free entertainment.

- **A handheld shower head is a useful gift.** It makes bathing a patient much easier and it's a great stress reducer, besides. Choose one with variable-speed massage pulse. These showers can provide pain relief and relaxation for tired caregivers, too. Take a peek in the family's shower to see if they already have one. If not, buy one and **install it for them.**

- **A monitoring device can give both patients and caregivers extra security.** This relatively inexpensive item ($30 to $40) enables the caregivers to hear, crystal clear, the patient from any other room in the home. Ask around among friends with school-age children. Many of them probably have a baby monitor already, just collecting dust on a closet shelf. Borrow one.

- **Arrange for and purchase a weekly housecleaning service for the family.** This is a wonderful gift for a group of concerned friends or co-workers to give.

- **Give time and expertise.** Those who can't make the commitment to offer regular weekly respite care can still stop by to make a *one-time* or a *specialty* contribution. Tell the spouse of an ill friend that you'll come over next Saturday from nine until four. The family should be prepared to keep you busy doing home maintenance projects all day—and of course, *you'll* make the runs to the hardware store. Or give the gift of planting and nurturing the patient's vegetable garden this year, turning over the bounty to the family.

- **Help with information gathering.** Offer up a weekend to make a trip to a university medical library for the family, to collect journal articles on the illness. Or give just one morning to make phone calls for the family, helping them get information about social services and their availability. See Navigating an Academic Library (p. 208) and Helpful Organizations (p. 211).

- **Do tedious paperwork for the family.** Help the family organize important documents. Write out their bills for them. Do their tax return. A really generous friend might even offer to file insurance claims for the family.

- **A birdfeeder is a fun gift,** especially the kind that attaches to the outside of a window with suction cups. It can be placed near a patient's favorite resting spot and can provide hours of relaxing entertainment. Don't forget the birdseed!

- **A cappuccino maker can be a special present** and a means to make the family's future visits from others a bit more festive. Unpack the appliance and learn to operate it yourself first, so you can teach the family to make their own lattes. (It's really very easy, but it can be intimidating if you have to carefully read the instructions and learn from scratch.) On later visits, you can bring a pound of flavored coffee and offer to make treats for the whole family.

- **These ideas are just a few of many. For others, gather friends and have a brainstorming party** (see Solving Problems the Creative Way, p. 127.)

- And remember—gifts can cost a fortune, they can cost nothing, but we've all known since we were children that the dollar amount isn't what makes the present priceless. **The most important gift we can give to families with illness is** *ourselves.*

NOTES

· 20 ·

SIGNATURES

When people ask me what this experience is like, the word that comes to mind is excruciating. Some things are so huge and intense I can barely stand it—like watching my husband and daughter and remembering, for the hundredth time, that they might be at her graduation without me. I can scarcely think about her wedding, or the grandkids I might never meet. Some things are too glaring and painful, like looking into the sun with your eyes wide open.

But excruciation isn't such a terrible thing—it makes things unbearably beautiful, too. Music. A certain shaft of moonlight. My husband singing in the shower. Sometimes I feel so full with how incredible life is, I literally want to scream with joy. It is a huge gift, this beautiful, complicated world. I want to shake people's shoulders until they see it, too. Maybe that will be my legacy—making them see.

· **Most people living with incurable illness would tell us—believe it or not—that there *are* a few fringe benefits to the experience.** Perhaps most rewarding, this journey helps us grow to deeply appreciate the world—and our place in it. We notice more. We take less for granted. We feel more passionate about life's beauties and tragedies. We grow impatient about wasting time. Often, the illness instills a strong need in us—even a calling—to contribute to the world around us.

- **Each person involved—the patient, his wife, his bowling team, his doctors, his business partner—leaves a personal imprint on this journey, a *signature* of sorts.** We leave our impressions—our histories and values and perspectives—on every other passenger we meet along the way. **And the journey itself leaves a lifetime signature on *us*.** Anyone closely connected to this experience can't help but be moved and changed by it. Helping a best friend through the illness of breast cancer, caring for an ill father for decades—these are powerful and rare life experiences. They are bound to change us, and ultimately these changes are for the better.

- **Living with illness encourages us to examine our personal legacies, to consider and even challenge the unique signature of our lives.** Are we compassionate? Generous? Have we accomplished all that we wanted? Are there any ancient hurts and angers lurking? If we died today, this very minute, how would we be remembered? And we come to appreciate, just like Ebenezer Scrooge, it's never too late to change.

- **In the most connected families, this illness gives everyone the push they need to examine their own signatures.** Together, we face the fact—everyone dies eventually. Some do it suddenly, some take more time; there are advantages and disadvantages to any calendar. When a death is sudden, suffering and fear are brief, but there's no opportunity for closure. With a slowly progressing death, suffering and fear may appear, be abated, then reappear, but for the patient and those who love him, there's also the chance that the circle gains control of the journey.

- **One of the best places to start, when surveying our personal signature, is to think about the important values and messages we hope to have instilled in others—the signature of our ethics.** A patient could write a letter like this one to those she loves:

_____

                                    Date

Dear Family and Friends,

I am grateful for _____

Something I am proud of is _____

What gives me most strength is _____

My most difficult time _____

My happiest memories _____

Something I regret is _____

The things important to me are _____

The values important to me are _____

The people important to me are _____

My wish for each parent _____

My wish for each child _____

My wish for each grandchild _____

My wish for each brother/sister _____

My wish for my spouse _____

My wish for these special friends _____

What I want people to learn from me is _____

What I want people to say about me is _____

                        With love and peace,

P.S. I also want you to know _____

_____

- **Such a treasure might be written for a whole group,** with scores
  of copies duplicated and distributed. Or it could be **handwritten
  and personalized,** for each member of a person's closest circle.
  It might be spoken into a **tape recorder.** Or spoken **in person.**
  Or **never spoken at all,** content to reside in our most private
  hearts.

- **In addition to the signature of our ethics, the experience of incurable illness inspires us to recall—and even record—the signature of our memories.** If a loved one expresses a need for help in getting started, here are ways to draw him out:

Firsts

My first car . . .
My first job . . .
My first day of school . . .
My first success . . .
My first failure . . .
My first best friend . . .
My first kiss . . .
My first trip . . .
My first major illness . . .
My first memory . . .
My first time away from home . . .

Growing Up

My hometown . . .
Growing up in _____(place)_____was . . .
Being born in the 20s (30s, 70s, etc.) meant that . . .
The house(s) where I grew up was . . .
Our neighborhood was . . .
When I was growing up, girls and women were . . .
When I was growing up, boys and men were . . .
As a child, some traditions that were always in place were . . .
On weekends we usually . . .
My earliest ambitions were . . .
Some childhood heroes were . . .
A secret place I had as a child was . . .
When I was little, I always dreamed that one day . . .
My parents usually disciplined me by . . .
I got in lots of trouble when . . .
My memories of my early school years are . . .

My favorite subjects in school were . . .
A favorite teacher was . . .
When I was little, something that really scared me was . . .
My favorite things to do as a kid were . . .
When I was a teenager, I used to . . .
The fashions of the day when I was young were . . .
When I was in college, I . . .
Some of my romantic interests have been . . .
Smells that remind me of my earlier years are . . .
Places I associate with my growing up are . . .
The special pets I remember are . . .
My best friends from elementary school were . . .
My best friends in high school were . . .
A childhood vacation I remember is . . .
A major embarrassing moment from childhood is . . .
A hard lesson I learned as a kid was . . .
A regret about my early years is . . .
When I was young, my family never knew I . . .
The people who helped me most when I was a young
        adult were . . .
When I was little, older people always said that I would . . .
When I was growing up, I always excelled at . . .
One of my fondest memories of childhood is . . .
As I've grown older I've changed, in that . . .

• When an important person is no longer in our life, we frequently look back and say, "There are so many things about him I never even knew. I never bothered to ask, and now I'm sorry." Incurable illness can motivate us to **share ourselves with each other while we still have the chance.** Here are some things to discuss and discover:

Favorites

My very favorite things to do . . .
My very favorite place . . .
My favorite hobbies . . .
My favorite sports . . .
My favorite foods . . .
My favorite movies . . .
My favorite books . . .
My favorite TV shows . . .
My favorite actors/celebrities . . .
My favorite songs . . .
My favorite people . . .
My favorite colors . . .
My favorite time of day . . .
My favorite day of the week . . .
My favorite season . . .
My favorite year . . .

My Family of Origin

My mother . . .
My father . . .
My siblings . . .
My grandparents . . .
Mother's family was . . .
Father's family was . . .
A favorite birthday celebration . . .
When I was little, we celebrated major holidays by . . .
My ancestry and ethnic heritage . . .
Our family's religious traditions were . . .
A favorite relative was . . .
A question I have about my family is . . .
The major values my parents tried to instill in me were . . .

The Family I've Made

When my spouse and I met . . .
I decided to get married because . . .
Our wedding was . . .
After my spouse and I had been married about ten years
    I . . .
Some of the major tests of our marriage have been . . .
When I had my first (and second, third, etc.) child, I . . .
When I was a young mother/father, I . . .
On holidays and birthdays we used to . . .
When the kids were little, I was really scared when . . .
Some funny or special stories about my children are . . .
Something about parenthood that has surprised me is . . .
Having kids during the 60s (50s, 30s, 80s, etc.) was . . .
When my children were teenagers I thought . . .
When I became a grandparent I . . .
The way I feel today about my marriage is . . .
The major values I've tried to instill in my children are . . .

World View

Of all the places I've visited, I have the most vivid memories
    of . . .
I still want to travel to . . .
Some of my strongest memories regarding current events
    are . . .
My most memorable U.S. presidents have been . . .
Some major political events have been . . .
The most exciting political time of my life has been . . .
Some political causes that have always been important to me
    are . . .
Community and volunteer work I've done is . . .
The income-producing work I've done is . . .
I would define my career by saying . . .
Some famous people I've met . . .
Some famous moments I've had myself are . . .

To me, *art* means . . .
The natural disasters I remember are . . .
The world changes I've seen are . . .
My wishes for the world are . . .

- We can also help family members share the **signature of life lessons,** which is enlightening to us and often a relief to them. We learn, and they gain support, when we talk about topics like these.

Peaks and Valleys

The best advice I ever received was . . .
My most embarrassing moment was . . .
I have always been better than others at . . .
The time I was most proud . . .
The most important experience of my life so far . . .
My major influences and mentors have been . . .
The biggest mistakes I've made have been . . .
The projects that have given me the most pleasure are . . .
The thing I've had to work very hardest at in my life is . . .
The one thing that makes me feel most alive is . . .
A major life regret is . . .
The hardest decision I've ever made . . .
One of the wisest things I've ever done is . . .
Some major hardships in my life have been . . .
The scariest time of my life was when . . .
The happiest times of my life have been . . .
The best thing I've ever done for someone else is . . .
The major blessings I've had are . . .

- **When sharing the signatures of our life experiences, it helps to get in the mood.** Listen to music from a particular era. Look through old photo albums. Take a drive with a friend or loved one past old haunts and houses. Call a long-ago roommate to reminisce.

- **There are lots of ways to record our signatures.** We can write out our responses to the items on the previous pages, or have someone else do the writing for us (or type our responses into a computer). We can speak into a tape recorder or a camcorder. Some people are more comfortable having a conversation with a friend who asks questions; some are happier to ask themselves the questions, performing this life review in private.

- **Being willing to share our life and its lessons is a beautiful legacy for our loved ones. And the sooner we start, the better.** Just imagine if we could hear our grandmother's voice when she was twenty, or hear our six-year-old singing his favorite song, fifty years into our family's future.

My father died when I was thirty-two, and there are so many things I now realize I never knew about him. It never even occurred to me to ask. And I'd give anything to have his voice on tape—he had the greatest voice and laugh—sometimes I miss his voice most of all.

My mother tells stories of her life all the time. I've heard them all so many times. I sometimes feel impatient and think, "I know. I've heard that one already." But if she died today I wouldn't remember half the details. Plus, no one can tell them the way she can. I've told her how hard it is, feeling like I've lost so much of Dad. So now she's taping her stories for us. She has a little cassette recorder beside her favorite chair, and she just sits there and talks. The last time I saw her she was a little sheepish. "I've used two ninety-minute tapes and I'm not even done with World War Two yet!" I told her, "I'm thrilled. Keep it up. I want everything you could ever say."

NOTES

REFLECTIONS:
ONE TRAVELER'S VIEWS OF
THE VOYAGE

It can be hard to catch your own reflection in these waters. When the boat moves quickly, it's risky leaning over the side; you can barely find a glimpse of yourself. And travel through turbulence, whether rapids or eddies, distorts your image. I suppose I ought to savor those times the river is slow and glassy, those moments I can safely stare into the currents of illness and see myself clearly reflected back.

I see myself together in this boat with my loved ones, but each of us takes a solitary journey. I can consider this river only from my own perspective. I know I'm supposed to empathize, to be concerned with how others are faring. But I get confused enough about my *own* resiliency; I try not to become overly anxious about my husband's reactions or our daughter's or those of friends and family.

Maybe that sounds hard-hearted or selfish, and in my own defense, I *do* keep a watchful eye on loved ones. But I also believe that each traveler is ultimately responsible for hanging on to the boat during this voyage. I don't think it's wise to lose my own grip just because I get nervous somebody else might fall overboard.

I think in Big Schemes; my husband thinks in Science and Statistics. (I tell him I always knew he was one in a million; the rarity of his illness now provides tangible proof.) He calls my hospice career a benefit; I call it a blessing. My family didn't have to start from scratch when seeking information and support. And because of my hospice work, our daughter had more exposure than most kids, years before illness appeared in our own family. These things help. Still, my professional calling is not without its ironies; even my closest friends and hospice colleagues can't help but comment on that.

For a time I stagnated in spiritual doubts about those ironies. I decided God knew, deep down inside, I was nothing more than a fake.

Sure, I wrote a book in 1992 that continues to be valued by hospice workers, and sure, I was flying around the country giving communication training to hospice workers. But in 1994, when my own husband was diagnosed with incurable lymphoma, I knew why. It was because God knew the *whole* truth. I was a sham, a charlatan, I didn't know my stuff. God gave my family this journey so I would finally deserve the career acclaim I had been fraudulently receiving.

Such an ego we can have, especially when faced with something so big as incurable illness. For a time, I half believed my own life controlled the universe.

Because of my work, the boundaries between personal and professional concerns get cloudy. It's disquieting sometimes, to give speeches and write books about how to do it for others, then look at my own reflection and face the ways I falter. I begin to question myself. I even consider the old adage I normally find offensive: "He who can't do, teaches."

My family copes with these boundaries issues, too. For over a decade I have been writing and speaking about families with illness; after my first book, *I'm Here to Help,* was published, I began this book—two years before illness happened to mine. It's odd to one day wake up and find your family living the manuscript. Sometimes it seems we can't get away from it. My loved ones are grateful this book is finally finished. I think they prefer it out in the world somewhere, instead of permeating the entire household.

And now, I have nearly completed one last hospice-related project—a companion piece to this volume, a book about dying, grief, and bereavement. Thankfully, not everyone holding this book on illness will require the sequel. (And I'm relieved to say I no longer egotistically think God will make my husband die just so my next book will be better.) Soon, I will be satisfied to move on. I've pondered long enough over illness, dying, and grief; it's time to get on to other things.

I'll write the novel I've planned since I was twenty. Plant flowers. Travel to Paris and London with my husband and daughter. Remind myself to savor the hundreds of things that can happen in a year—a gift I appreciate more, now that my family no longer takes a year for granted.

To close, I offer a heartfelt wish. When you're floating down this river, find a quieter time to lean over the side of your craft. Look at your face in the water. May you find laugh lines. May you see peace and dignity. And deep inside your eyes, may you find a flicker of wisdom: There is more to life than its final chapter.

NOTES

APPENDIX

·

These pages contain medical and clinical information for the layperson. They are designed to give readers confidence and skill in the physical elements of care and to inspire friends and acquaintances to offer caregiving respite to the patient families they know.

A detailed outline of each chapter and its contents, in lieu of an index

EMERGENCIES

When in doubt, call for help. Check the inside cover of the patient care notebook for appropriate **emergency phone numbers**. Many families wisely put these numbers on stickers, then **put a sticker on every telephone in the house**.

If the family is receiving hospice care, instruct respite caregivers to **contact the *hospice* in any emergency, rather than phoning 911.** If 911 is contacted, a crew of people who do not know this family will come to the house, engage in CPR, and rush the patient to the hospital in an ambulance. They are *required by law* to do this, although these actions might run counter to the wishes of the family. **Hospice is available twenty-four hours a day and can help guide you through situations/problems that arise.**

THE PATIENT CARE NOTEBOOK

Patient family members as well as respite caregivers are far more confident when they can refer to the three-ring binder where the family keeps everything relevant to the patient's physical well-being. Having all this information handy in one place will greatly expedite information sharing among all these people—professional and otherwise—who love and care for the patient.

- *The inside cover contains medical emergency numbers with twenty-four-hour response, plus names and numbers of other family members and of friends who should be notified immediately.*

- *One section lists all medications (dosages, reactions, changes); a running tabulation of every medicine the patient ingests.*

- *Another section lists doctors, nurses, home health aides, with their phone numbers, voice mail, and faxes.*

- *A third section contains brief notes of each medical visit, new prognosis information, etc.*

- *In a fourth is treatment information, any special instructions regarding administration, side effects, and so on.*

- *Yet another area contains medical and insurance records—account numbers and information, bills and receipts.*

- *Finally, there is a section on general care—nutrition, bathing, skin care, etc., or any handout provided by the medical team.*

You can buy books like these (I've seen one called *Patient Pal* for $19.95), or you can inexpensively make one of your own from materials found at any office supply store. Just buy a three-ring binder, a three-hole punch, and some dividers, and you're set.

THE ABCs OF PHYSICAL CARE

It isn't really that complicated to care for a seriously ill person. Most of it is common sense. As you consider making this commitment, consult the following pages to provide confidence. While primary caregivers are probably already aware of these basics—they've learned them from their medical team or through trial and error—these bytes of information might prove comforting to a friend or loved one who agrees to provide respite. Take this information with you while you stay with the patient. The experience won't be nearly as scary as you think.

Aphasia   The patient may have an inability to process language, either verbal or written. She has difficulty either understanding others or expressing herself; sometimes she has trouble with both. Speech is disjointed, twisted; the person may swear or say things unknowingly. Nonverbal methods may work best (pointing to objects); speak slowly; simplify vocabulary; ask questions that can be answered with a yes or no; reinforce messages through repetition; continue to speak calmly, never loudly; make sure the person looks at your face when you speak; do not correct speech; encourage the patient to say things a different way if you do not understand.

Bathing   Baths can be very calming and wonderful for pain management, in addition to being necessary for hygiene. If you stay with the patient longer than one night, learn how to give a bath. Practice in the presence of the primary caregiver or a home health aide first. Become comfortable transferring the patient back and forth to the bath; this can be a dangerous part of the job. A bath chair and handheld shower will expedite the bathing. Make sure the chair is stable and all soaps and linens are gathered before beginning. Be thorough but relatively speedy (unless the patient wants to soak, for pain-relief purposes). If the patient is relatively mobile, turn away to give him privacy while he washes the genital area. You can make this clinical and nonembarrassing by simply handing over a clean, wet (not soapy) cloth while saying, "Here's a cloth to wash the privates, if you like." Then find something else to occupy your attention. From start to finish, be sure the room is very warm. Afterward, dry the patient thoroughly and apply a mild fragrance-free lotion. To avoid a chill, help the patient get dressed in the bathroom, if there is room.

To give a bed bath   Wash in parts; concentrate on the face, hands, underarms, genitals, and feet. Use a very warm, damp cloth, not soapy unless absolutely necessary. Premoistened wipes can be used if you feel deep cleansing is required (but they irritate some skin, and they will be cold; warm them in your clean hands, first). Afterward, rinse with a warm, wet cloth. Dry thoroughly as you go; each area can also be protected with lotion. Keep the room warm and cover all parts of the body that are not being currently washed to avoid chill. If the patient is ambulatory, provide privacy so she can wash her own genitals. If not, gently but thoroughly do so for her. **For patients who are especially shy or private**, it is perfectly acceptable to wear a swim suit or T-shirt while having a bath. Suggest this as an option. And it is completely possible to wash a body without directly looking at it.

Bedsores   Skin breakdown is one of the caregiver's main concerns; it can happen very quickly when people are bedridden. These painful little skin ulcers are difficult to heal, and once present, great care must be taken to keep them from enlarging. It helps if the patient sleeps on an egg-crate or sheepskin mattress, over which is placed a spotless cotton bottom sheet, the softer the better. The more a patient can move and circulate, the less the risk of bedsores. Several times a day, sit the patient up with legs dangling over the sides of the bed, to get the blood flowing. If the patient is very weak, turn him every three or four hours—from side to back to other side. Range of motion exercises can also improve circulation. Prevent skin from touching other skin, where it can rub and chafe. Put a pillow between the legs, a towel between the arms and torso. Keep a careful watch for red spots, especially in places where skin touches bone (on a thin ill person, there will be many such places). Look at heels, knees, head, the tops of ears, the tailbone, pelvic bones. If you see any evidence of a bedsore, regardless how small, let the medical team know as soon as possible. There will be immediate treatment—perhaps salve, padding, special bandages that also enable airflow. The faster a bedsore is attended, the less the risk of serious problems. *A day can matter.*

Breathing   As discussed elsewhere, the patient's breathing may sound irregular, even alarming and scary. *Ap-*

nea—the temporary cessation of breathing—is a common occurrence in seriously ill people. The patient may use oxygen; hopefully the unit has a humidifier attachment to decrease drying effects. Keep a careful watch on the tanks and your supply. You might use portable units for taking short trips with the patient. Be sure to pad the tubing that goes over the ears to prevent irritation; use soft cotton or gauze. Use Vaseline to coat and protect the lips and nose near the tubing. Remove the nasal prongs occasionally, to provide a break. Patients occasionally need more and more oxygen as the illness progresses. If your loved one seems to struggle more than usual for breath, if she has a sudden decrease in her energy for talking, speak to the medical team about increasing her oxygen. However, *never* increase the oxygen without first consulting the medical team (in some situations, increasing oxygen even though someone is short of breath can be very dangerous). Many patients with respiratory-related illnesses are especially afraid—the fear of suffocating and the inability to pull in air are among the most terrifying experiences we can have. If the patient is in distress because she feels like she can't breathe, call the medical team. While you wait for their advice, try putting the patient's bed at a forty-five-degree angle. If the patient has been prescribed a nebulizer, and it is within the prescribed time frame, give an application to open the airways. Opening a window or positioning a light fan to blow across the patient's face can also help; it increases the sensation of airflow and hospice nurses have found this can reduce the patient's anxiety.

Catheter   When a patient is incontinent or urine elimination is a problem, a catheter may be used. Tubing is inserted through the urethra into the bladder so that elimination can occur continuously and spontaneously. The catheter will be inserted and maintained by a home-care nurse, hospice nurse, or physician who can be contacted with any questions, concerns, or problems.

Constipation   This is a very common and uncomfortable side effect of many medications, coupled with changes in nutrition and the body's decreasing ability to digest. Over seventy-five percent of all hospice patients need treatment for constipation. Certain pain management medications can really increase this problem. For instance, most hospice professionals would never start a regimen of aggressive pain relief without also prescribing a proactive approach toward constipation. A diet heavy in fruit can help. Typically, bowels should move every one to three days; this comfort level is frequently accomplished by using a laxative *regularly,* even when constipation isn't a problem. Hospice research finds that the number one cause of constipation is that patients take the medication sporadically rather than regularly. If regular laxatives aren't enough, some patients can add a daily program of milk of magnesia. An enema will also provide relief. Severe constipation might actually look like diarrhea. There may be a light leaky feces, but this is actually just a dripping past the larger, solid obstruction. The fecal material can also be removed manually by medical professionals, though this can be painful and the patient should be sedated.

Incontinence The problems associated with bladder and bowel control are typically much more troublesome to the patient than they are to the caregiver. Though we may think this would be the worst part of it all, cleaning up after the occasional accident typically becomes routine. Make things easier by using a protective covering between the mattress and the sheet (never put protective covering in direct contact with the patient's skin). When accidents occur, it is essential to clean the bedding and the patient completely and immediately. The ill person's skin is very fragile; it mustn't be exposed to the harsh chemicals of urine and feces. Complete the job by airing the environment. An important point: Interpersonal reassurance is the most important skill of all. Make sure the person knows the situation is no big deal and that it is quite normal (because it *is*). And if the patient ever seems uncomfortable or is shifting around in the bed or chair, tactfully check the bedding and underclothes. There may have been an accident and the person is too shy to say so.

Infection Control Use careful and proper handwashing techniques any time you touch the patient or her belongings. Use warm water, lather well with firm rubbing, loosen dirt on palms, between each finger, knuckles, under nails, around rings. Rinse extremely well, pat dry with a clean cloth or paper towel. Use universal precautions adopted from the medical industry. Use gloves whenever touching anything "liquid" or expelled by the patient, including urine and fecal material, open sores, mucous membranes, blood. Disposable surgical gloves are available at any pharmacy, relatively inexpensive and usually sold one hundred per box (they fit either hand); you'll learn to love them for lots of household tasks, not just patient care.

Insomnia Sleep disturbances are common for seriously ill people, but they are often more problematic for caregiver than patient. Sleep reversal is typical—the patient dozes through the day but is awake throughout the night. Recurrent nightmares can be a problem; it helps to gently discuss them and try to find meaning in them. Sometimes, patients are afraid to go to sleep, with fear that they might not wake up. It can help for a caregiver to sleep in the same room with the patient; some patients have even been comforted by having a bell nearby, or even holding a string to the sleeping caregiver's hand so they can summon help instantly. The causes of insomnia can be many—the disease state, medications, anxiety about approaching death, even something as basic as lack of exercise. Insomnia increases when the patient is bored or inactive during the day; encourage the patient to do light range of motion exercises, walking, and isometrics. Ask if the patient would be comfortable in a chair and move him there during part of the day. At bedtime, institute a calming nightly ritual. Provide a warm, nurturing snack (not liquid). Quiet the environment, dim the lights. Read softly together. Straighten the bed in a routine fashion, offer a back rub up to the count of twenty. A major antidote to insomnia is medication. If the person wakes to take a four-hour dose of pain medication, ask the medical team about doubling the bedtime dose.

Mobility   One of the major physical changes a person experiences as illness progresses is loss of mobility. A walker and wheelchair may be needed, and the patient isn't always open to these new modes of transportation. If you will be caring for a seriously ill person for a half day or more, ask for training in transferring the person from bed to a walker, or from walker to commode. Practice using the wheelchair, maneuvering it around tight corners and over obstacles like doorjambs and curbs. Try pulling it *backward* over any hump in the path, rather than pushing the patient over it, going forward. Learn to tilt the chair back a bit, so you can roll it safely but comfortably on its two rear wheels; this increases mobility. Whenever physically moving or lifting the patient, take extra care to protect your *own* body, in addition to his; never lift in a way that could damage your back. Ask for training in the specific methods for turning a patient, moving him upward or downward in bed, and so forth.

A FEW PRINCIPLES OF PATIENT TRANSFER:

• **It is generally easier to push than to pull.**

• **Always arch the small of your back** (in a pronounced fashion—really stick out your bottom) whenever you are lifting the patient, pushing or lifting anything heavy, or otherwise straining your body.

• **Use your knee to save your back.** Whenever you need to turn or move the patient in bed—and even when doing something so minor as stretching to make the bed—get in the habit of placing your knee up on the bed beside you. This position automatically forces you to arch your back.

• **Try to think of becoming one unit with the patient** when moving and transferring her. Use your bodies to complement each other; use each other as levers and pulleys in the same machine.

• **In general, keep your feet (and the patient's) pointed in the direction you wish to move.**

• **Whenever supporting the patient, make sure your feet are firmly planted and your weight is evenly distributed between them.** The farther apart your feet, the harder it will be to throw you off balance.

• **Move the patient in stages, and the tighter the package, the easier** the person is to move. For instance, when moving the patient upward in bed, first pull his knees up and place his heels close to his buttocks. Then stand at the head of the bed, grasping the patient firmly but gently under the armpits, and pull upward, toward you. Straighten sheets and bedclothes.

• **To move a patient from a lying to a sitting position** (the first step of getting him out of bed), first roll him on his side, facing the edge he will eventually exit. Pull his legs out and down over the edge; as the legs go down, firmly support his shoulders while using your upper body to lift his upper body to a sitting position. It may help to have the head of the bed raised.

• **To move from a sitting to a standing position,** once the patient is sitting upright with her legs dangling over the edge of the bed, place her feet firm and flat on the floor, evenly spaced, as far back under her center of gravity as possible. If her feet slip or she has little motor control and strength to keep them in place, use *your* feet to brace and position *hers*. Place the walker directly in front of her, or turn your *own* body into a walker by holding your upper arms taut and perpendicular on either side of the patient. The patient firmly grasps the walker (or your taut, outstretched arms), and with a tiny one-two-three and boost from you—remember to keep your back arched!—she is up, painlessly for you both.

• **To move from a standing to a sitting position**—as in moving to a commode or in the first step of returning to bed—walk the patient as close as possible to the bed. With the walker or yourself as support, have the patient turn around so that the backs of her legs press against the edge of the bed. Have her lean forward on the walker and work her feet backward, so that they are fully under her center of gravity. Using your strength and her upper arms, she lowers herself to a sitting position.

• **To return from sitting to lying down in bed,** the patient simply leans on her side until her upper body is resting solidly on the bed; if the bed is in a raised position, this might be easier. Once her upper body is secure and resting, lift her legs and place them on the bed. Then, straighten sheets and bedclothes as you help the patient roll onto her back.

• **A transfer belt is a handy device that makes moving together much safer.** The patient wears a wide, sturdy belt loosely around the waist; the caregiver can use it to hoist up a patient, and even more important, she can grab the belt instantly to prevent a fall. Transfer belts are available at medical supply stores. Actually, any strong belt or lashing strap from your camping supplies will do.

Mouth Care   The mouth is prone to pain and infection during serious illness. It becomes dry through mouth breathing and certain medications, and the patient has difficulty producing saliva. It needs careful hygiene. Brush the teeth twice per day; three times, if there is an infection. Throughout the day, use a baking soda or saline rinse to cleanse the mouth and provide artificial saliva (1 tsp. baking soda to 1 quart water; or 1 tsp. salt to ½ quart water). Serve food tepid. Warm up cold food, and cool down hot foods before serving. The patient should wear dentures during the day—if comfortable—to retain jaw alignment. Dentures should be removed and cleansed every night, during sleep.

Nausea/Vomiting   Seriously ill people will frequently need to make an adjustment to their internal conditions. Certain foods, smells, or medications can produce feelings of nausea and result in vomiting. Contact the medical team when this occurs; be prepared to let them know what foods, activities, and other conditions seemed to accompany the behavior. After vomiting, gently rinse the mouth. Offer to brush the patient's teeth, if she would like. Or use a rinse, saline or baking soda. After nausea, the patient can take small sips of herbal or black tea (no milk). Liquids should be clear and tepid. When the person can begin to handle solids, provide small frequent meals, without a lot of liquid. Aroma therapy (adding a particularly pleasing fragrance to the environment through oils, candles, incense, etc.) can sometimes help a person relax when she is experiencing waves of nausea.

Nutrition   This area is one of the more complex and psychologically difficult for patients and caregivers alike. Spiritually and intellectually, we tie our very survival to food, and now the loved one is eating quantities that seem alarmingly minuscule. He may ask for a regular meal, then find he can only eat a bite. At first, this is just as distressing to the patient as it is to caregivers. He wonders, "What's wrong with me? Why can't I eat like I used to?" Soon, the patient begins to accept the ever-diminishing appetite, but caregivers frequently make the mistake of pushing the patient to eat and drink more. We caregivers are so emotionally tied to our loved ones, we just can't bear to watch them do something preventable like starve themselves to death. We say things like, "You *have* to eat. You'll never be able to get well if you don't have proper nutrition. *Eat!*" This pressure only makes the situation worse. **Do not nag the person to eat more.** His body is shutting down its appetite *on purpose.* Instead, try to increase appetite through increased activity. Also avoid serving hot liquids like tea or cocoa before meals; these can diminish the appetite. Serve five to six small meals a day, rather than three overwhelming plates full of food. Keep lots of Jell-O and pudding on hand, for easy-to-digest, easy-to-eat refreshing snacks. To enhance nutrition, add powdered nonfat dry milk to soups and casseroles. Choose attractive foods that are easy to chew and digest. Give the person plenty of time to eat and drink. Don't rush. The patient may need help with eating; it's more work than you might imagine, to raise a spoon to your lips twenty times. Many liquids (soups, coffee, even ice cream) can be most easily sipped through a straw. Most important, allow the patient to decide about eating and drinking—what, when, and how much.

Phantom Limb   This phenomenon of being able to feel a body part that has been removed is very real. While scientists are not precisely sure why it happens, they know it *does.* Amputees and women who have undergone mastectomy often report a sensation in the missing arm, leg, or breast. If the patient is comfortable with the idea, it can help for a caregiver to massage the area where the removal occurred. The medical team might have additional advice for treating phantom discomfort; let them know what you are experiencing, even if it seems crazy.

Seizures   Periods of spasmodic activity can be terrifying to an uninitiated caregiver. But seizures might be relatively common, especially for patients with brain tumors, neurological damage, or fever. If a seizure occurs, lay the person down on a safe, padded surface. (Blankets and bedspreads on the floor work well.) Turn the head sideways to keep airways open and facilitate vomiting, should that occur. If the patient is in bed, pad the siderails with blankets and towels. Contrary to popular belief, do *not* put anything between the teeth of a person having a seizure; this might damage his teeth, tongue, or jaws. Contact the medical team and stay with the patient throughout the episode. Afterward, if it is possible to easily transport the person back to bed, do so. Otherwise, keep him comfortable and covered, with pillows and blankets on the floor, until help or advice arrives.

PAIN AND ITS MANAGEMENT

• **Pain is real, even if no one can find a reason for it and even if the person experiencing it looks and acts fine.** Do not doubt your perceptions of your own pain, and do not let others tell you whether it is real. How would *they* know?

• **Patients and caregivers alike need to be careful about "fudging."** Never hide painful symptoms because you don't care to bother others; never give any patient a reason to think you won't believe her.

• **It goes without saying, any person (incurable or not) can experience more than one pain at the same time.** The average hospice patient manages four separate discomforts, usually successfully. We need to assess each pain *separately.*

• The first thing to determine is whether a particular pain is **chronic or acute**. An acute pain is generally sharp or pronounced, and it goes away with time. A deep cut on your finger is a good example; mastectomy is another. Chronic pain is there continually; it will not cure itself or go away. The pain of arthritis is an example; the pressure of internal tumors against organs is another. Both are manageable, but the methods are different. Acute pain is likely to react well to interventions (like medications) given in response to pain; chronic pain needs interventions (like medications) on a continual basis.

• **People live so long with chronic pain they eventually develop the ability to function normally, at least most of the time. That's why medical professionals sometimes say insensitive things,** such as "You seem to be okay whenever *I* see you," or "I can't find any reason for this pain." Even more distressing is when they say, "There's nothing we can do about your pain."

• **Do *not* resign yourself to living in pain.** Many health care practitioners, plain and simple, don't have expertise in pain management; they may honestly believe there is no help available.

• **Instead, turn to experts and organizations who specialize in pain control. Contact the hospices in your area.** Even if you are not eligible for hospice care, you can get help with pain management. Hospices specialize in the topic and at the very least can provide referral information. And perhaps you could even make arrangements to hire a hospice professional to visit with you periodically, as a consultant. Ask for advice on how to proceed.

• **Family members can also look in the Yellow Pages for pain clinics. Contact organizations that help people with especially painful diseases.** Call the Cancer Information Service, the American Cancer Society, or other appropriate national organizations. Also contact pharmacologists, oncologists, anesthesiologists, neurosurgeons, and psychologists in your region. *Do not give up.*

• **Acute and chronic pain will likely respond to medication, both over the counter and prescription.** Much of your pain management consists of trying drugs in different combinations, working until you find the right blend that seems to control discomfort with the fewest damaging side effects. For a good introduction to the medications available, see *The Hospice Movement* by Stoddard and *Dying at Home* by Sankar. As these books demonstrate, pain management can be complex. The patient needs professional monitoring on a regular basis.

• **While you do your research on medications and their side effects, stop to stomp out a few harmful myths about pharmaceuticals. First, pain medication cannot be "used up."** A person does not have to live in pain now because "I have to save the pills for later, so there will be enough when I *really* need them." When something stops working, the pain medication will be *changed*. Dosages will be increased, entirely new meds will be substituted. Take your medications, now.

• **You will not become addicted to narcotics used for pain management.** Experts have seen, time and time again, patients discontinue narcotics like morphine with no withdrawal symptoms. Addiction occurs in less than one percent of all incurable patients, according to researchers affiliated with Sloan-Kettering Cancer Center. Unfortunately, this addiction myth has caused much unnecessary pain. Many patients with histories of chemical dependency are undermedicated during illness because patient/family members are scared about "stirring up old problems again." Patients and loving onlookers must be assertive to ensure this doesn't happen.

• **"If I feel better, I can stop taking the medications." . . . Wrong!** Pain medications, especially those that control chronic pain, are used in a preventative sense; patients need to take them in a "plan ahead" way. If you take small doses on a regular, continual basis, the pain may subside completely, and you really don't need much medication to accomplish this. Your primary pain medications must be taken around the clock; they should not be prescribed as PRN (take when needed). Sometimes, patients experience **breakthrough pain**—the intensity of a chronic pain increases, or a new acute pain occurs. In these cases, your medical team will likely prescribe additional PRN medications, tell you to increase the dosages of your primary medications, or both.

• **Pain medications might be pills and syrups, but not always. Sometimes a particular condition makes oral medications impossible; caregivers may need to learn how to give injections.** Try not to be anxious about this; you will get lots of help, and the whole process will probably be much easier than you expect, especially when you can provide relief to your loved one. **Another common form of pain control, particularly in a hospice setting, is the pump, an intravenous form of continual, controlled medication** whereby morphine is released directly and regularly, and the patient has the option of administering an extra dose when needed.

• **Caregivers and loved ones can help the patient assess her pains and document them in a journal: symptoms, duration, and methods used for re-** lief. Help her take her medications as prescribed. Help her perform the additional nonnarcotic pain-management techniques in this book. Maintain a close relationship with the medical team, to ensure their rapid response to any new developments such as breakthrough pain or new symptoms.

• **Last, keep the patient focused on** *now.* It won't help to worry that the pain will get worse later, perhaps as a tumor gets larger. Just work on controlling it *today.*

ASSESSING PAIN

• **To control pain, you'll need a detailed assessment and one that requires constant monitoring and updating.** This important job must not be taken lightly. The assessment will document, as precisely as possible,

  • the **location** of each pain

  • a **description**

  • its **duration**

  • its **changes**

  • what measures (if any) currently provide **relief**

  • and if possible, a probable **cause**

• **Locating the pain is often accomplished through body charts, which can just be front and back drawings of the human body.** The patient draws the specific pain locations, noting on the chart which pains are external, which are internal, which are closer to the surface, which are deeper.

• **The medical team will also ask you what level of pain is tolerable to you. A frequent request is that you describe the pain on**

a scale of 0 to 10—with 0 being no pain and 10 being the worst possible. For instance, you rank your back pain at this moment a "7"; you rank it an "8" at its very worst (at night) and a "5" at its least. Your current goal is to make it a "2" and everyone's ultimate goal is to make it a "0."

- **Describing pain isn't easy. Use as many adjectives as you feel necessary to convey the sensations. Here are a few descriptive words to get you started.** Check all the ones that seem to apply; there may be many. Consider the pain in terms of its *movement*, its *pressure*, and its *temperature*.

flickering	*quivering*	*pulsing*	*throbbing*
beating	*pounding*	*jumping*	*flashing*
shooting	*pricking*	*boring*	*drilling*
stabbing	*lacerating*	*sharp*	*cutting*
pinching	*pressing*	*gnawing*	*cramping*
crushing	*tugging*	*pulling*	*wrenching*
tight	*numb*	*squeezing*	*taut*
splitting	*tender*	*tearing*	*piercing*
penetrating	*dull*	*sore*	*achy*
itchy	*stinging*	*smarting*	*tingling*
hot	*burning*	*scalding*	*searing*
freezing	*cool*	*cold*	*shaking*

- **Also document the intensity of each pain, as well as its buildup and duration. Which of these descriptions apply?**

nagging	*irritating*	*annoying*	*strong*
mild	*moderate*	*weak*	*exhausting*
spreading	*increasing*	*decreasing*	*inescapable*
excruciating	*severe*	*agonizing*	*comes in waves*
suffocating	*grueling*	*growing*	*just noticeable*

- **Document duration:**

5 minutes or less?	several hours or less?
1 hour or less?	several days or less?
1 day or less?	continual?

- **Document other activities when it occurs:**

  before or after eating?   when active?
  when at rest?   when in a certain position?
  time of day it occurs?   other noteworthy observations?

The medical experts who help your family with pain management will ask you these questions and more. They may also ask if the patient finds relief with any **nonnarcotic, noninvasive measures, such as the ones described below.** (For more information on these and other techniques, see also Therapies for Stress and Burnout, p. 139.)

RELIEVING PAIN

- **Start with the deep-breathing techniques** (diaphragm breathing, rhythmic breath control) described under Therapies for Stress and Burnout, p. 139. Have a caregiver sit with the patient and breathe with her in a slow, deep rhythm. Softly say "one" on each inhale, "two" on each exhale, to provide the patient with an audible focal point.

- **Combine breathing with isometrics** (the isolated tensing, then relaxing, of specific parts of the body). On each inhale, tense a certain part of the body and hold the breath to the count of ten. On each exhale, relax that body area. Then wait ten seconds and move on to another part of the body. Start with the crown of the head and work all the way to the toes. If the caregiver softly says, "tense" during inhale and "relax" during exhale, the patient can focus more easily.

- **Distraction techniques can be very effective, but only for pain that is short-lived, five to forty-five minutes in duration, maximum.** Distraction can be very helpful when the patient is waiting for other pain medications to take effect. Some techniques are reading a novel, watching a movie on tape, engaging in a hobby like needlework or model making, an easy game of cards, gentle socializing.

- **Music can be an effective distraction tool, especially when pain is intense.** Listen to fast music, rather loud, through headphones. Concentrate on using part of your body to tap out the rhythm to every song. Once this forty-five minute tape is over, you will hopefully be through this pain.

- **Skin stimulation techniques are easy for caregivers to help administer, and they can be extremely helpful.** Experts believe it is possible to interrupt pain impulses through changing pressure and temperature on the skin, because the same nerve endings are used to convey all three messages (pain, temperature, and pressure) to the brain. Therefore, if you make a radical change to temperature or pressure, the brain becomes busy dealing with this new information—it blocks out the pain impulse. Skin stimulation also alters blood flow to the area of treatment. It should be used with extreme caution by patients with skin weakness and lesions. Patients who have received radiation should also take care. Some methods of skin stimulation are

  - **Heat**—relieves sore muscles, provides all-around feelings of comfort and security. Use a heating pad in small doses (not more than one to two hours per time), never at night and never on bare skin. Also avoid heat over a new injury (it can increase bleeding) or an area numb to feeling. Take care if using heat with patients drowsy from medication or otherwise unable to convey their sensations.

  - **Cold**—used less frequently than heat, perhaps because it doesn't seem as nurturing. This is unfortunate because it can be very effective in numbing a wide variety of pains; it is often more helpful than heat. Obtain lots of "gel-paks" to keep in your freezer; they are available at any pharmacy or medical supply store. Wrap these in towels and place on painful areas. Stop if the patient starts to shiver or if the cold itself creates discomfort.

  - **Pressure**—Experiment applying pressure directly on or near the area of pain; use the heel of your hand, your thumb, knuckle, or fingertip. Start by applying pressure for ten seconds; if it seems to help, use the technique for a full minute. This can provide relief from minutes to hours.

- **Vibration**—Hold a handheld vibrator directly over or near the painful area. Give a head massage or lower-back massage with vibration. A bed vibrator can be a good investment for patients with all-over muscle ache.

- **Menthol Rubs**—Many over-the-counter products can be rubbed into the skin to provide the sensations of heat and cold. These wonderful concoctions can numb the pain completely, sometimes providing several hours of relief per application. Test a small one-inch area with the menthol. If the skin doesn't become irritated, lather it on in bigger doses. These rubs typically contain an aspirinlike ingredient, so *be sure to tell your medical team* you're using them. And sometimes, a particular brand will lose its effectiveness; try switching to another with slightly different ingredients if the patient develops a tolerance. And of course, never use any chemical like this over broken skin, or a rash, near the eyes, or near any mucous membrane area (mouth, genitals, rectum).

- **Massage**—Refer to Therapies for Stress and Burnout, p. 139, for techniques. Needless to say, a massage for a very ill person might need to be light and stroking, rather than penetrating. Ask the patient what feels best. Use a nonalcohol-based lotion, oil, or talc to keep from drying out the skin. Most patients prefer something that is fragrance free. They may be very sensitive to smells and react with nausea or respiratory distress.

- **Circle Stroking**—Very lightly rub rapid small circles in the palm of the patient's hand. Other good spots are the tummy and the small of the back. Your touch is extremely light and gentle, almost unnoticeable. Combine this touch with breathing exercises you talk through and perform with the patient. The circle strokes provide a very relaxing focal point.

- **TENS**—A transcutaneous electrical nerve stimulator is a device that applies a mild current to selected parts of the body, sometimes directly on or near a painful area, sometimes symmetrically opposite to it. This interferes with the pain impulse and can provide a pleasant tingling sensation in place of pain.

- **Acupuncture**—The ancient practice of placing needles in certain pain-control areas of the body has proven helpful for many people in pain. Take care with acupuncture if receiving chemotherapy; there could be a danger of increased bleeding where the needles are placed.

- Imagery exercises, such as those in Therapies for Stress and Burnout (see p. 139), can be useful in achieving overall relaxation. **When using imagery for specific pain control, try also creating pictures that are transformational.** In other words, use your images to *change* the pain. If the pain feels hot, imagine packing it with more and more snow, feel it get colder and colder. Or imagine a ball of fire growing smaller. Or "good" cells gathering in waves, smothering the "bad" cells of illness.

- **Use relaxation tapes**—listen to New Age music or to tapes with breathing or muscle-relaxation instructions. Check with your library, a good bookstore, music store, and your medical team for ideas and selections.

- **Most patients can be kept quite comfortable through using a variety of these techniques, combined with a well-educated team that manages and closely monitors *aggressive* pharmaceutical care.** Obviously, pain management methods sometimes *cause* symptoms as well as alleviate them; patients experience constipation, insomnia, or nausea. For information on these problems, see The ABCs of Physical Care, p. 193.

- The important thing for now is **don't give up. Get relief. The patient does not have to experience debilitating pain.**

RESEARCHING THE ILLNESS AND OPTIONS

It doesn't really matter what a family knows, at this moment. A more important matter is what can they find out? And how efficiently?

- **Start your research by asking lots of questions of the physicians and other medical experts on your medical team.** Ask for copies of journal articles, bibliographies, pamphlets, organizations, etc.

- **Periodically ask to review the medical file.** Copy all the pages and keep your own duplicate file at home. Ask to be copied on any memo, fax, report, or letter about the case. (Note: This won't always be easy; physicians can be reluctant to release the patient's file and written documents, but they must if we insist. It's the law.)

- **Make phone contact and get on the mailing lists of any organizations** that are pertinent to the family's situation (see Helpful Organizations, p. 211).

- **Get connected on the Internet.** Look for other patients with similar experience; search for resources, answers, and assistance.

- **Visit the biggest public libraries available. Better yet, make a trip to an academic library** connected to a university medical school. Find a few friends or loved ones who would be willing to devote a weekend, and possibly travel several hundred miles. It can be well worth it. It is here we find the actual journal articles that describe ongoing research written by the scientists actually doing that research. Public libraries, even the huge ones, mostly have only the *People* magazine or *Popular Science* versions of an illness.

NAVIGATING AN ACADEMIC LIBRARY

Before you go, telephone. Locate the university's main number through directory assistance (area code +555-1212). Ask the university's main switchboard to connect you to the medical school library and ask

- *What hours are you open? When are you least crowded?*

- *Can anyone use the library? Even non-students? What restrictions apply?*

- *How do I get there? What parking is available? At what cost?*

- *What duplicating services are available? At what cost?*

- *Are any other facilities nearby? Cafeteria? A park? A museum?*

- *I'm traveling a long distance to do this—what else do I need to know before I arrive?*

Also contact the local chamber of commerce for information about lodging, transportation, attractions (for family members who accompany you, and for relaxing after a full day's work at the library).

- **Plan to visit the library for one to two days.** The first visit (or morning), use the computer to print out bibliographies. The second visit (or afternoon), collect articles and make photocopies of them.

- **Never sit and actually *read* at the library; reading is far too time-consuming.** Feel free to briefly skim articles and abstracts, but keep focused on the main goal—to amass the most information in the shortest time possible. When we stop to read, we get distracted and have less time to collect other articles. Later, back at home or at the motel, there will be plenty of time for reading.

- **Never walk into a library as if you know what you're doing. That only wastes valuable time.** Instead, head straight to the main information area and immediately put yourself in a librarian's capable hands by stating precisely why you are there. Just explain, "A family member has been diagnosed with a serious illness called XYZ. I'm here to make copies of all the important and recent articles that have been written about XYZ and its treatment." The **librarian will show you how to use the computer—an electronic card catalog databank that can list and print a bibliography of all available articles** about any illness. The librarian will explain which keys move you through the entries, how to tag the articles you want, and finally, how to print out your list. There may be a nominal per page charge for printing these bibliographies.

- **To create these bibliographies, we need to supply the computer with keywords about the illness, so it will know to highlight *only* those articles in a specific area of interest;** for instance, using a keyword like *cancer* is far too broad; thousands and thousands of articles would be listed. **Come prepared with the proper spelling of a specific diagnosis, be prepared with a list of symptoms, be able to correctly spell any treatment options or other illness-related words** the medical team has mentioned.

- Every once in a while, the computer will print out an **abstract—a detailed description of an article's contents, generally one to three paragraphs.** If an abstract is well written, it includes a good overview of the research and findings, as well as any reservations or questions about the findings. **Abstracts save**

a tremendous amount of time, because a person can learn a lot about the illness through reading a short synopsis, rather than having to wade through an entire article. *The more abstracts you can collect, the better.*

• At the end of a sedentary first visit, you'll have pages of bibliographies and abstracts. At the **second visit, you will be more active, walking the stacks to collect and photocopy all those articles listed. Head straight for the information desk again, for an overview of how this particular library is organized.** The shelves will be arranged in alphabetical/chronological order—and each of your article titles has a particular letter/number combination that corresponds to its specific location on the shelves.

• **It is much faster to collect the articles as they are arranged in the library, rather than how they are arranged on the printed bibliography.** It wastes lots of time to walk for the first article listed on the printout, then the second, then the third, and so on. Instead, go through the entire list and collect all the articles beginning AAA-CCC, check them off. Then go through the entire list to collect and check off all the DDD-GGG articles. Then, HHH-LLL, etc.

• It helps to have two workers on this second trip: a finder and a copier. **The finder retrieves the articles, using a small scrap of paper to mark an article's place** in the big leather journals that bind them. The finder carries the heavy leather volumes over to **the copier, who feeds quarters into the machine and photocopies all the pages.** Note: Many libraries have a duplicat-

ing service; for a per page fee the library might be able to copy all these articles for you, often a worthwhile investment.

• **Helpful tools: A clipboard,** to hold bibliographies. **Highlighters,** to mark articles found, missing, or categorized in other helpful ways (for example, all articles about the illness are highlighted in green, the ones on treatments are pink). **Coins and small bills,** for the copy machines, for vending machines. **And a reminder—no reading!**

• Once the library has given all it has to offer, the researchers return home with stacks of articles. This can be intimidating (there's so much to digest!) and comforting (you'll be able to make truly informed decisions). Use the trick of graduate students everywhere—**skim. Search only for main points, not detail.** Carefully read the introduction, then the conclusion, then the first and last sentence of every paragraph. But force the eyes to move very quickly over the rest of the text. **Use a highlighter when you read** to isolate new vocabulary words for the family glossary, to emphasize main points about the illness, treatment side effects. The highlighting will also make the article easier to understand for future readers. As you read, **think of questions. Write them down immediately** in the margins and on a separate piece of paper. Collect them to take to appointments.

• **Not every family member needs to get involved in obtaining and reading this literature—too many helpers may only confuse the issue.** Give the job only to those people who are good at it. Have them condense the information for others.

HELPFUL ORGANIZATIONS

Contact a reputable self-help clearinghouse. These organizations maintain extensive lists of the nation's thousands of self-help groups and resources. Just tell them a few specifics about your situation, and they can let you know what groups and resources might be available in your area. Each will charge you a small fee ($6 – $15) for their services, to cover printing and postage. A few numbers to try:

- *American Self-Help Clearinghouse*
  (201) 625-7101

- *National Mental Health Consumer Self-Help Clearinghouse*
  (800) 553-4539

- *The National Self-Help Clearinghouse*
  (212) 354-8525

Below are phone numbers for a wide variety of specific organizations that could prove helpful to a family living with illness. They are listed alphabetically; be sure to scan the entire list because your area of interest might be represented in several different places. Some organizations may prove more accommodating than others. Be sure to ask each person you speak with for referrals of other people and organizations to contact.

- **AIDS** Clinical Trials Group, National Institutes of Health (301) 496-8210 *U.S. government program coordinating testing of experimental treatments for AIDS*

- **Al-Anon Family** Group Headquarters (212) 302-7240

- **Alcoholics Anonymous** World Services (212) 870-3400

- **ALS** Association (Lou Gehrig's Disease) (800) 782-4747

- **ALS** and Neuromuscular Research Foundation (Lou Gehrig's Disease) (415) 923-3640

- **Alzheimer's Disease** & Related Disorders Association (800) 272-3900

- American **Amputee** Foundation (501) 666-2523

- American **Art Therapy** Association (708) 949-6064

- American Association of **Kidney** Patients (800) 749-2257

- American Association for **Marriage and Family Therapy** (202) 452-0109

- American Association of **Pastoral Counselors** (703) 385-6967

- American Association of **Retired Persons** (AARP) (800) 424-2277 *Offers free pamphlets, info on caregiving, Medicare, etc.*

- American **Cancer** Society (800) ACS-2345

- American **Chronic Pain** Association (916) 632-0922

- American Council of the **Blind** (800) 424-8666 or (202) 467-5081

- American Council for Drug Education (800) 488-DRUG *information on **prescription drugs***

- American **Diabetes** Association (800) ADA-DISC

- American Foundation for the **Blind** (800) AFB-LINE or (212) 502-7600

- American Foundation for **Urologic Disease** (800) 242-2383

- American **Heart** Association (800) 242-8721 or (214) 373-6300

- American **Liver** Foundation (800) 223-0179

- American **Lung** Association (800) LUNG-USA

- American **Lupus** Society (310) 542-8891

- American **Paralysis** Association (800) 225-0292

- American **Paralysis Association Spinal Cord Injury** Hotline (800) 526-3456

- American **Psychiatric** Association (202) 682-6000

- American **Psychological** Association (202) 336-5500

- **Anxiety Disorders** Association of America (301) 231-9350

- Betty Ford Center (619) 773-4100 *substance abuse* support

- **Cancer** Care (212) 221-3300

- Chemocare (**Cancer**) (800) 55-CHEMO *matches cancer patients with volunteers who have had similar diagnosis*

- Children's **Leukemia** Research Association (516) 222-1944

- **Chronic Pain** Support Group (216) 526-1530

- **Cocaine Anonymous** World Services (800) 347-8998 or (310) 559-5833

- Compassionate Friends (708) 990-0010 *bereavement* support

- Courage **Stroke** Network c/o Courage Center (800) 553-6321

- **Crohn's and Colitis** Foundation of America (800) 932-2423

- **Cystic Fibrosis** Foundation (800) FIGHT-CF

- **Depression and Related Affective Disorders** Association (410) 955-4647

- Families Anonymous (818) 989-7841 *substance abuse*

- Foundation for **Depression and Manic Depression** (212) 772-3400

- **Hospice Nurses** Association (412) 687-3231

- **Kidney Transplant/Dialysis** Association (617) 267-3747

- L. E. Support Club *Lupus Erythematosus* (803) 764-1769

- **Leukemia** Society of America (800) 955-4LSA

- Living Bank (800) 528-2971 *information on* **organ donation**
- **Lupus** Foundation of America (800) 558-0121 or (800) 800-4532
- **Medicare** Hotline (800) 638-6833
- Mothers of **AIDS** Patients (619) 544-0430
- **Multiple Sclerosis** Foundation (954) 776-6805
- **Muscular Dystrophy** Association (520) 529-2000
- National **AIDS** Clearinghouse (800) 458-5231
- National **AIDS** Hotline (Ctr Disease Control) (800) 342-AIDS
- National Alliance of **Breast Cancer** Organizations (NABCO) (212) 719-0154
- National Alliance for the **Mentally Ill** (800) 950-NAMI
- National **Amputation** Foundation (516) 887-3600
- National Association for Children of **Alcoholics** (301) 468-0985
- National Association of **Hospital Hospitality Houses** (800) 542-9730 or (317) 288-3226 *housing for families of patients undergoing long-term treatment*
- National Association for **Music Therapy** (301) 589-3300
- National Association for Parents of the **Visually Impaired** (800) 562-6265 or (617) 972-7441
- National Association of **Social Workers** (202) 408-8600
- National **Cancer** Institute, CIS (800) 4-CANCER
- National **Chronic Pain** Outreach Association (301) 652-4948
- National Council on **Alcoholism and Drug Dependence** (800) NCA-CALL or (212) 206-6770
- National **Family Caregivers** Association (301) 942-6430

- National **Health Information** Center (800) 336-4797
- National **Heart, Lung, Blood** Institute Information Center (800) 251-1222
- National **Hemophilia** Foundation (212) 219-8180
- National **Home Caring** Council (212) 674-4990 *for info about in-home services*
- National **Hospice** Organization (800) 658-8898 or (703) 243-5900 *for information about hospice programs in your area*
- National Institute of **Mental Health** (800) 421-4211
- National Institute of **Neurological Disorders and Stroke** (301) 496-5751
- National **Insurance** Consumer Helpline (800) 942-4242
- National **Kidney** Foundation (800) 622-9010
- National **Kidney and Urologic Diseases** Information Clearinghouse (301) 654-4415
- National **Mental Health** Association (800) 969-NMHA
- National Minority **AIDS** Council (202) 544-1076
- National **Multiple Sclerosis** Society (800) FIGHT-MS
- National Organization for **Rare Disorders** (800) 999-6673
- National **Parkinson** Foundation (800) 327-4545
- National **Spinal Cord Injury** Association (800) 962-9629
- National **Stroke** Association (800) STROKES
- Parents Helping Parents (408) 727-5775 *Care, services, and education for **special needs kids** and their families*
- **Parkinson's** Disease Foundation (800) 457-6676
- **Parkinson** Support Groups of America (301) 937-1545
- Ronald McDonald Houses (708) 575-7418 ***housing for families** of patients undergoing long-term treatment*

- **Sickle Cell** Disease Association of America (800) 421-8453 or (310) 216-6363

- **Social Security** Administration Hotline (800) 772-1213 or (800) 325-0778 (TTD)

- **Spina Bifida** Association of America (800) 621-3141 or (202) 944-3285

- **Suicide and Crisis** Hotline (800) 333-4444 *24-hour service*

- Systemic **Lupus** Erythematosus Foundation (212) 685-4118

- United **Parkinson** Foundation (312) 733-1893

HELPFUL READING

These books are just some of many that might be helpful to families living with illness. Phone ahead to your library or favorite bookstore to be sure a particular title is on the shelf. If not, most good bookstores will be willing to order it for you.

Achterberg, Jeanne, Barbara Dossey and Leslie Kolkmeier, *Rituals of Healing: Using Imagery for Health and Wellness.*

A wealth of practical insight and treatment for all sorts of illness pain, physical and otherwise.

Ahronheim, Judith, and Doron Weber, *Final Passages: Positive Choices for the Dying and Their Loved Ones.*

Questions for doctors, pain control, depression, hospice and comfort care, health care and financial planning, expressing feelings.

Aladjem, Henrietta, *Understanding Lupus: What It Is, How to Treat It, How to Cope with It.*

Written by one of the founders of the Lupus Foundation of America.

Amenta, Madalon, and Nancy Bohnet, *Nursing Care of the Terminally Ill.*

The award-winning classic, thorough, definitive, and guaranteed to instill confidence in any practitioner.

Beissler, Arnold R., *A Graceful Passage.*

Essays and personal reflections on living and the right to die, how and when one chooses.

Benson, Herbert, and Miriam Klipper, *The Relaxation Response.*

Information and techniques of meditation, helpful for stress reduction in patient families as well as for hospice workers.

Beresford, Larry, *The Hospice Handbook.*

What hospice is, what it isn't, asking the right questions, finding hospice care; an early classic in the field of hospice.

Berg, Elizabeth, *Family Traditions: Celebrations for Holidays and Everyday.*

A nonfiction work, practical and beautifully presented, for families who wish to enhance life.

Berg, Elizabeth, *Talk Before Sleep.*

A beautiful novel about a hospice situation and the handful of friends who experience it together. Also by Berg, *Range of Motion,* a novel about a young wife and mother whose husband lies in a coma; the book provides insights and inspiration about medical expertise and family connections.

Berman, Claire, *Caring for Yourself While Caring for Your Aging Parents.*

How to help and survive, including long-distance caregiving, only children, finances.

Blau, Sheldon Paul, with Dodi Schultz, *Living with Lupus: All the Knowledge You Need to Help Yourself.*

A more personal guide, less clinical than Wallace but perhaps more helpful philosophically.

Bluebond-Langner, Myra, *The Private Worlds of Dying Children.*

Based on Ph.D. research—a nine-month study in a pediatric hospital—the author covers knowing and concealing information, the causes and consequences of mutual pretense, and more.

Broyard, Anatole, *Intoxicated by My Illness and Other Writings on Life and Death.*

A beautiful book—eloquent, compact, unsentimental, and rich.

Buscaglia, Leo, *The Fall of Freddy the Leaf: A Story of Life for All Ages.*

A tale of the life of a leaf, with full-color photos; good way to orient kids to life's cycles.

Callanan, Maggie, and Patricia Kelley, *Final Gifts.*

A beautifully written book that tunes us into appreciating the symbolic communication and metaphors used by patients with Nearing Death Awareness; can enhance patient-family relationships.

Canfield, Jack, and Mark Victor Hansen, *Chicken Soup for the Soul: 101 Stories to Open the Heart and Rekindle the Spirit.*

Inspirational stories by and about famous people. See also *A 2nd Helping of Chicken Soup* and *A 3rd Helping of Chicken Soup,* and keep eyes open for future helpings.

Carlson, Richard, and Benjamin Shield, editors, *Handbook for the Soul.*

A collection of writings by well-known theologians (Robert Fulgham, Wayne W. Dyer, Ram Dass).

Carroll, David, *Living with Dying: A Loving Guide for Family and Close Friends.*

Helpful, solid information, reader friendly, written in a question-answer format.

Carter, Rosalynn, with Susan K. Golant, *Helping Yourself Help Others.*

A helpful definition of caregiving, excellent resources lists—pages of organizations and bibliography, by condition.

Chapman, Elwood N., *The Unfinished Business of Living: Helping Aging Parents Help Themselves.*

A reader-friendly workbook approach to the pragmatics of caregiving and planning.

Childs-Gowell, Elaine, *Good Grief Rituals: Tools for Healing.*

Short, sweet, and pragmatic; ideas to immediately implement, for finding hope, healing, and meaning.

Chopra, Deepak, *The Seven Spiritual Laws of Success,* also *The Way of the Wizard* and several other books that provide Eastern perspectives and insights.

Cooke, Margaret, with Elizabeth Putnam, *Ways You* Can *Help: Creative, Practical Suggestions for Family and Friends of Patients and Caregivers.*

This tiny little book is full of wonderful "why didn't I think of that" gems. It gives readers instant ideas for offering tangible support. (It covers things like new babies, too—which proves especially uplifting.)

Cousins, Norman, *Anatomy of an Illness as Perceived by the Patient: Reflections on Healing and Regeneration.*

A personal testimony of the healing powers of laughter, courage, and persistence, coupled with a strong doctor-patient relationship.

Cousins, Norman, *Head First: The Biology of Hope and the Healing Power of the Human Spirit.*

A demonstration of author's beliefs that optimism and strong doctor-patient relationships can ease the pain of illness and increase chances of survival. Based on author experience, interviews with doctors, patients, scientists.

Davis, Martha, Elizabeth Robbins Eshelman, and Matthew McKay, *The Relaxation and Stress Reductions Workbook.*

An excellent and in-depth presentation of many stress-management techniques, helpful to any caregiving family.

Donoghue, Paul J., and Mary E. Siegel, *Sick and Tired of Feeling Sick and Tired: Living with Invisible Chronic Illness.*

Emotional support for the special circumstances of living with a hidden or invisible illness.

Duda, Deborah, *Coming Home: A Guide to Dying at Home with Dignity.*

A highly practical, comforting, and inspiring guidebook for home caregivers—a great book for patients and families.

Duff, Kat, *The Alchemy of Illness.*

A from-the-heart book that seeks healing and celebrates the special insights and awareness gained only by living with illness.

Eidson, Ted, editor, *The AIDS Caregiver's Handbook.*

Not quite as clinically thorough as the Greif/Golden book, but with more philosophical-meanings focus.

Feinstein, David, and Peg Elliott Mayo, *Rituals for Living and Dying.*

How we can turn loss and the fear of death into an affirmation of life; a book of tools, insights, and stories.

Fisher, Mary, *I'll Not Go Quietly.*

Talks by the famous AIDS patient/activist.

Fisher, Mary, *My Name Is Mary.*

The author/activist's most recent work, her memoirs.

Fisher, Mary, *Sleep with the Angels.*

More talks by the patient/activist.

Ford, Michael Thomas, editor, *The Voices of AIDS: Twelve Unforgettable People Talk About How AIDS Has Changed Their Lives.*

Fry, Virginia Lynn, *Part of Me Died, Too: Stories of Creative Survival Among Bereaved Children and Teenagers.*

Helpful and beautifully written narratives of children experiencing grief.

Galanti, Geri-Ann, *Caring for Patients from Different Cultures.*

An enlightening anecdotal account of culture and sensitivity in a medical setting.

Graham, Judy, *Multiple Sclerosis: A Self-Help Guide to Its Management.*
A clinical, thorough discussion.

Gray, John, *Men Are from Mars, Women Are from Venus.*
The bestseller about improving interpersonal communication, particularly between the sexes.

Greif, Judith, and Beth Ann Golden, *AIDS Care at Home: A Guide for Caregivers, Loved Ones and People with AIDS.*
An excellent handbook, full of information especially about physical care.

Grollman, Earl A., A prolific and charismatic rabbi and psychologist who specializes in grief. Some of his many titles include: *Living When a Loved One Has Died; Talking About Death: A Dialogue Between Parent and Child;* and *Straight Talk About Death for Teenagers: How to Cope with Losing Someone You Love.*

Gruetzner, Howard, *Alzheimer's: A Caregiver's Guide and Sourcebook.*
The pragmatic day-to-day realities of living with Alzheimer's.

Imber-Black, Evan, and Janine Roberts, *Rituals for Our Times: Celebrating, Healing and Changing Our Lives and Our Relationships.*
An in-depth overview of rituals with exercises for creating them, examining the self, and finding new meaning.

Irish, Donald, with Kathleen Lundquist and Vivian Nelson, *Ethnic Variations in Dying, Death and Grief.*
One of the first comprehensive volumes on culture and dying.

Kabat-Zinn, Jon, *Full Catastrophic Living: Using the Wisdom of Your Body and Mind to Face Stress, Pain and Illness.*
Written by an expert in meditation, stress reduction, and managing chronic pain.

Kabat-Zinn, Jon, *Wherever You Go, There You Are: Mindfulness Meditation in Everyday Life.*
Insights and methods for increasing joy, depth, and awareness.

Karnes, Barbara, *Gone from My Sight: The Dying Experience.*

A pithy pamphlet that outlines the physical and mental changes that occur as death approaches, from a few months or weeks, to just days, hours, and minutes beforehand. Send $2.00 to Barbara Karnes, P.O. Box 335, Stillwell, KS 66085.

Karnes, Barbara, *A Time to Live: Living with a Life-Threatening Illness.*

A short and comforting pamphlet for newly diagnosed people. Send $2.00 to Barbara Karnes, P.O. Box 335, Stillwell, KS 66085.

Keirsey, David, and Marilyn Bates, *Please Understand Me.*

Information on Myers-Briggs.

Kramer, Kay, and Herbert Kramer, *Conversations at Midnight: Coming to Terms with Dying and Death.*

A married couple's dialogues about living with illness; the wife is a social worker specializing in grief work, the husband a communications consultant who has incurable cancer.

Kubler-Ross, Elisabeth. Perhaps the most renowned—and controversial—expert on the subject of death and dying, Kubler-Ross is also a prolific writer on the subject, beginning in the sixties with her classic *On Death and Dying* and more recently with *AIDS: The Ultimate Challenge.* Her numerous books are unique, from interviews and poignant photojournalism to highly technical, clinical descriptions. Her voice is penetrating and far-reaching.

Kushner, Harold S., *When Bad Things Happen to Good People.*

The classic bestseller that has already helped millions find peace and meaning in life's tragedies.

Lang, Susan S., and Richard B. Patt, *You Don't Have to Suffer: A Complete Guide to Relieving Cancer Pain for Patients and Their Families.*

Over-the-counter meds, prescriptions, opioids and nonopioids, their effects and side effects, plus information on alternative methods of pain management.

Larkin, Marilynn, *When Someone You Love Has Alzheimer's: A Dell Caregiver Guide.*

A practical paperback covering behaviors, finances, physical care, and more.

Larson, Dale G., *The Helper's Journey.*

Excellent information on caregiver stress and self-care.

Lerner, Harriet Goldhor, *The Dance of Intimacy, The Dance of Anger, The Dance of Deception.*

A trio of great insights, family therapies, and genogram information.

LeVert, Suzanne, *When Someone You Love Has Cancer: A Dell Caregiver Guide.*

A practical little paperback covering all facets of living, caretaking, planning.

Levine, Stephen, *Meetings at the Edge.*

Dialogues with the grieving and dying, the healing and the healed; a good source of psychological/philosophical support.

Levine, Stephen, *Who Dies?*

A predominantly philosophical investigation of conscious living and conscious dying.

Lieberman, Abraham N., and Frank L. Williams, *Parkinson's Disease: The Complete Guide for Patients and Caregivers.*

A thorough, clinical overview.

Mace, Nancy L., and Peter V. Rabins, *The 36-Hour Day: A Family Guide to Caring for Persons with Alzheimer's Disease, Related Dementing Illnesses and Memory Loss in Later Life.*

Extremely thorough and clinically helpful.

Markin, R. E., *The Alzheimer's Cope Book: The Complete Care Manual for Patients and Their Families.*

A brief and practical book, comforting as it orients the family toward the effects and pragmatic decisions of Alzheimer's.

Martz, Sandra, editor, *If I Had My Life to Live Over I Would Pick More Daisies.*

More stories and poems, this time focusing on women and their life choices.

Martz, Sandra, editor, *When I Am an Old Woman I Shall Wear Purple.*

Stories, poems, and photographs of and by women who see life and aging as gifts.

McGoon, Dwight C., *The Parkinson's Handbook.*

An inspiring, practical guide by a Mayo Clinic surgeon who lives with Parkinson's.

McGowin, Diana Friel, *Living in the Labyrinth: A Personal Journey Through the Maze of Alzheimer's.*

A short and heartfelt testimonial.

Montague, Ashley, and Floyd Matson, *The Human Connection.*

A look at interpersonal communication from an anthropological, biological, sociological standpoint.

Moore, Thomas, *Care of the Soul.*

A warm and comforting book that encourages us to find depth and sacredness in everyday life. And more recently by Moore, *Soul Mates—Honoring the Mysteries of Love and Relationship.*

Morse, Melvin, with Paul Perry, *Closer to the Light.*

A groundbreaking bestseller that put the notion of the near death experience (NDE) into our vernacular and made us all consider just how wonderful dying might feel.

Morse, Melvin, with Paul Perry, *Transformed by the Light.*

Continued research on people who have had NDEs shows them to be profoundly changed for the better, for the rest of their lives, with greater peace, zest for living, less fear of death.

Moyers, Bill, *Healing and the Mind.*

In book form, the famed PBS series appears as interviews and articles by experts the world over, who explore the mind-body connection and its healing powers.

Nuland, Sherwin B., *How We Die: Reflections on Life's Final Chapter.*

A physician's descriptions of body-system shutdowns, from deaths of various causes.

Osis, Karl, and Erlendur Haraldsson, *At the Hour of Death.*

A clinical overview of the death experience; deathbed visions, apparitions, depression, and pain, back from death experiences. Good source citation.

Patton, Marvyl Loree, *Guide-Lines and God-Lines for Facing Cancer.*

A spiritual and practical book about living with serious illness; inspiring, not preachy.

Pollin, Irene, with Susan K. Golant, *Taking Charge: How to Master the Eight Most Common Fears of Long-term Illness.*

A clear and extremely helpful book that covers self-image, abandonment, dependency, loss of control, anger, isolation, as well as improved communication with family members and doctors.

Polster, Erving, *Every Person's Life Is Worth a Novel.*

A book that encourages and motivates us to celebrate and tell our own stories.

Powell, Lenore S., with Katie Courtice, *Alzheimer's Disease: A Guide for Families.*

This book's strength is the emotional rather than clinical support it offers caregivers.

Quenk, Naomi L., *Beside Ourselves: Our Hidden Personality in Everyday Life.*

Insights on Myers-Briggs.

Quindlen, Anna, *One True Thing.*

A gripping novel about a woman caring for her dying mother; she's later accused of euthanizing her; excellent insights into family dynamics and ethics of incurable illness.

Rando, Therese, *How to Go on Living When Someone You Love Dies.*

A classic text on loss and surviving it, from one of the nation's most respected experts.

Rando, Therese, *Parental Loss of a Child.*

The expert author focuses on one of the more painful and difficult grief situations.

Rando, Therese, *Treatment of Complicated Mourning.*

A more recent contribution, warmly written yet highly clinical and helpful.

Redfield, James, *The Celestine Prophecy.*

The bestseller that has intrigued millions to consider connections — energy, power, the past, the future.

Register, Connie, *Living with Chronic Illness: Days of Patience and Passion.*

A poignant book with its main focus on philosophical meanings.

Rinpoche, Sogyal, *The Tibetan Book of Living and Dying.*

A spiritual classic that opens us to new ways of thinking and being, from one of the foremost interpreters of Tibetan Buddhism to the West.

Rosen, Eliot J., *Families Facing Death: Family Dynamics of Terminal Illness.*

Rosof, Barbara D., *The Worst Loss: How Families Heal from the Death of a Child.*

This book pays attention to relationships between child and parents, also between parents as partners; some helpful information on children's grief.

Rudd, Andrea, and Darien Taylor, editors, *Positive Women—Voices of Women Living with AIDS.*

A collection of writing, poetry, and interviews with thiry-seven women with AIDS who hail from all over the world.

Ryder, Brett, *The Alpha Book on Cancer and Living.*

A reader-friendly overview with a family focus; it runs the gamut, from medical science to "meanings."

Sachs, Judith, *When Someone You Love Has AIDS: A Dell Caregivers Guide.*

A handy paperback, full of clinical information, other resources, and more.

St. James, Elaine, *Simplify Your Life: 100 Ways to Slow Down and Enjoy the Things That Really Matter.*

A small and simple book, but poignant, spiritual, and ever so practical; a great gift for the right caregiver or patient.

Sankar, Andrea, *Dying at Home: A Family Guide for Caregiving.*

Well written, practical, lots of information on physical care, helpful to a medical novice caregiver.

Sarton, May, *A Reckoning.*

A poignant novel that traces the final year of Laura Spellman, who is diagnosed with inoperable lung cancer. She takes over the helm of her illness and comes to terms with her life and her relationships.

Sheehan, George, *Going the Distance: One Man's Journey to the End of His Life.*

A poignant and inspiring book by a well-known cardiologist and runner coping with cancer.

Sheridan, Carmel, *Failure-Free Activities for the Alzheimer's Patient: A Guidebook for Caregivers and Families.*

This tiny book is crammed with ideas we can instantly use to interact with Alzheimer's patients, from crafts to cooking and beyond; the book's ideas can provide hours of joy for patients and families.

Sherry, Michael M., *Confronting Cancer: How to Care for Today and Tomorrow.*

Overview of cancer and its main types, its treatments and pain management; of caregiving, planning, and putting affairs in order.

Spiegel, David, *Living Beyond Limits: New Hope and Help for Facing Life-Threatening Illness.*

Weathering the diagnosis, taking time, fortifying families, dealing with doctors, controlling pain, among other chapters.

Staudacher, Carol, *Men & Grief.*

When challenged by workshop participants that "men grieve differently; talk about *us,* too" the author decided to research gender and grief. She provides interview information, talks about roles of husband and father.

Stoddard, Sandol, *The Hospice Movement: A Better Way of Caring for the Dying.*

An early and important classic about hospice care and its development.

Stone, Richard, *Stories: The Family Legacy, A Guide for Recollection and Sharing.*

A brief and beautifully produced pamphlet on methods for drawing out the stories in those we love; contact Story Work Institute (407) 767-0067.

Tannen, Deborah, *You Just Don't Understand* and *That's Not What I Meant.*

A sociolinguist looks at language use, with major emphasis on gender differences; a forerunner to John Gray.

Thomas, Richard, *Multiple Sclerosis: A Comprehensive Guide to Effective Treatment.*

Succinct, practical, and easy-reading excellence; a great orientation.

Von Oech, Roger, *A Kick in the Seat of the Pants* and *A Whack on the Side of the Head.*

Two highly practical, helpful, and fun books on creativity and idea generation. Also available as a *Whack Pack*—a handy deck of Tarot-sized cards, each with a different creativity tip, idea, or sparkler. Use the cards at family meetings.

Wallace, Daniel J., *The Lupus Book: A Guide for Patients and Their Families.*

Thorough and clinical.

Williams, Gene B., and Patie Kay, *The Caregiver's Manual: A Guide to Helping the Elderly and Infirm.*

An informative book about all aspects of home care—physical, legal, emotional, with particular emphasis on the elderly patient.

Worden, William, *Grief Counseling and Grief Therapy.*

A classic examination of the grief process, quite clinical yet warmly written, accessible to the layperson.

Zakarian, Beverly, *The Activist Cancer Patient: How to Take Charge of Your Treatment.*

An excellent book that helps readers research their illness; lots of excellent how-to tips, as well as in-depth discussion of cancer and treatments.

Zunin, Leonard M., and Hilary Stanton Zunin, *The Art of Condolence.*

What to write, say, and do for others at their time of loss.

HOME-CARE EQUIPMENT: MAIL ORDER

Home care can be so much easier with the right equipment—maybe the patient could use special pillows, eating utensils with bent or foam handles, tonglike reachers, or other tools for daily living. Many of these things can be homemade (a handle can be built up for easier grasping with masking tape or pipe insulation) and such tools might not be covered by insurance. But perhaps the perfect item is available and even inexpensive, through a mail-

order company like the ones below. Call for catalogs, and phone your library for names of other companies.

- Sears Medical Catalog (800) 326-1750
- Self-Care Catalog (800) 345-3371
- Communication Aids for Children and Adults (Crestwood Company) (414) 352-5678
- Healthhouse USA (516) 334-9754
- Dr. Leonard's Healthcare Catalog (908) 225-0880
- Home Health Products for Life (800) 284-9123
- The Safety Zone (800) 999-3030

CHRONOLOGY OF CONTENTS

A detailed outline of each chapter and its contents, in lieu of an index

ACKNOWLEDGMENTS

I wish to acknowledge and give thanks to the following for their help and expertise in completing this book: For her tact, humor, and efficiency, editor Sandi Gelles-Cole. For their belief and persistence, agents Gail Ross and Howard Yoon. For her exacting eye, copyeditor Katherine S. Balch. To the entire team at Bantam Books, who were thorough, supportive, and compassionate, with special thanks to Toni Burbank for her overall clarity of vision and especially to Brian Tart, who never once left my psychological or spiritual side, even though we're physically thousands of miles apart. To my beautiful daughter, Kelley, age nine, for finding the title. And last but not least, to my friend and colleague Nancy Gelle, RN, Hospice Manager, Methodist Hospital Hospice, who lent her expertise to the technical/medical sections in this book and who has helped me in other major ways, long before now.

And to those who loved me anyway, even while I was writing it: My family, especially sister Marion Ray Kriwanek. My friends, especially Jan Steffen and Cathe Kobacker. And most of all, Doug and Kelley.

ABOUT THE AUTHOR

M. Catherine Ray is a hospice educator, author, and volunteer. She provides workshops all over the nation and is a frequent presenter at conferences hosted by the National Hospice Organization. Catherine holds a B.A. magna cum laude in interpersonal communications, and a master's degree in speech communication. Since 1977 she has taught college-level courses in interpersonal communications, negotiation, and public speaking.

In 1984 Catherine began to specialize in hospice communication, traveling throughout the region to provide hospice workers with training in patient family communication. Her articles and book reviews have appeared in *Hospice Magazine, Fanfare,* and the *American Journal of Nursing.* After becoming a hospice volunteer herself, Catherine was ready to write *I'm Here to Help: A Hospice Worker's Guide to Communicating With Dying People and Their Loved Ones.* This book is used by hospices all over the nation to train their staff and volunteers in patient family communication.

After completing *I'm Here to Help,* Catherine's immediate dream was to write an expanded version — for patients and loved ones rather than those who help the family professionally. *I'm With You Now* was begun in 1993. A year later, Catherine's husband was diagnosed with a rare lymphoma. She hopes her family's experience with incurable illness is enlightening rather than self-indulgent.

Catherine lives with her husband and daughter near Minneapolis. The family enjoys travel, boating, biking, and music.